Turning Your Man
Into Putty
in Your Hands

Turning Your Man Into Putty in Your Hands

Susan Wright

A Citadel Press Book
Published by *Carol Publishing Group*

A Citadel Press Book
Published by Carol Publishing Group
Citadel Press is a registered trademark of Carol Communications, Inc.

Editorial Offices: 600 Madison Avenue, New York, N.Y. 10022
Sales and Distribution Offices: 120 Enterprise Avenue, Secaucus, N.J. 07094
In Canada: Canadian Manda Group, P.O. Box 920, Station U, Toronto, Ontario M8Z 5P9

Queries regarding rights and permissions should be addressed to Carol Publishing Group, 600 Madison Avenue, New York, N.Y. 10022

Carol Publishing Group books are available at special discounts for bulk purchases, for sales promotions, fund raising, or educational purposes. Special editions can be created to specifications. For details contact: Special Sales Department, Carol Publishing Group, 120 Enterprise Avenue, Secaucus, N.J. 07094

Manufactured in the United States of America

10 9 8 7 6 5 4 3 2 1

Library of Congress Cataloging-in-Publication Data

Wright, Susan (Susan G.)
    Turning your man into putty in your hands / Susan Wright.
        p.   cm.
    "A Learning Annex book."
    "A Citadel Press book."   ISBN 0-8065-1455-8
    1. Sex instruction for women.   2. Men—Sexual behavior.
I. Title.
HQ46.W75   1993
306.7'07—dc 20   93–20610
                                             CIP

Contents

Introduction

Would you like to be able to turn your man into putty in your hands? You won't get what you want by just waiting for the "right" man to come along—one who innately possesses the unique combination of attitudes, words, and actions that you desire. Your needs are very specific, whether you're involved in a long-term relationship, or marriage, or going on a first date. You may not have examined your own desires in depth, but you recognize and are drawn to men who give you what you need. So why not take control and make sure your man gives you what you want?

How to Turn Your Man Into Putty in Your Hands examines the development of men and women's expectations, both from themselves and from one another; and shows how that knowledge can help affect your real relationships. You'll be given ways to find out what you really want from a lover and then shown how to go about getting it. Since mating and sexuality go hand in hand, paths to free and individual sexual expression are also explored. In the last section of this book, there are specific questions that I've received in response to my "Ask Susan" column in *The Learning Annex Magazine*. These letters illustrate particular problems and provide practical solutions to getting what you want from your lover.

Defining a "Good Relationship"
The first thing that must be done in order to take control of anything—whether it's a relationship, your lover, or your

life—is defining and understanding your own needs and desires. Complex and contradictory as those often are, you have to explore, accept, and trust your feelings and intuition. Understanding yourself gives you the confidence to get what you need from situations and people. In a larger sense, the better you know your own responses, the easier it will be to turn the world into putty in your hands, much less a man.

If a friend were to ask if you would like to have a good relationship with a man, or a better relationship with the man you have, you would probably answer yes and define it no further. You have relationships with your friends, with your family, with your doctor, with your coworkers. In some relationships—with your hairstylist, for instance—you define the type of service you want quite clearly, and you don't waste much time changing hairstylists if you don't get it.

People usually don't define what they want from relationships with friends. Time is spent with people who like to spend it in ways similar to the ways you do. You talk to the people who understand your point of view and your likes and dislikes, and with time, if your personalities are compatible, a friendship grows. But think about it—you spend little time discussing the nature of your "relationship" with your friend. You don't need to, because you take it one day or one activity at a time.

Friendships aren't plotted out, and that's acceptable because your future doesn't depend on any one friendship in particular. However, the quality of your future does depend in part on the lover in your life. Inevitably, you have expectations of a person who might become your mate because you have a desire for a certain type of future for yourself.

To get that future, you have to determine continually what your needs are. Define what type of person you desire in your life right now—one who will help you get what you need and who will give you the type of attention and sexual interaction that you see as love. Is it casual, or is it committed? Make a detailed list—not just the daydream or fantasy qualities of your perfect man in the perfect scenario between the two of you—be realistic as well. Look at your friends. What qualities do they have that makes them close to you? Obviously, you desire those things in people. What qualities have attracted you to past lovers, and what qualities do you want to avoid? What qualities about yourself do you most admire?

This is an ongoing process. As you transform and mature, your needs will change as well. If you are in a long-term relationship, you'll have to continue to make your desires known to your lover as you both change and grow.

Compromise is often helpful: You can be flexible in the ways you get what you need. But don't ever compromise your desires themselves. You are what you want; if ultimately you don't get that, the relationship is not what you need. Then nothing can keep it from shattering, regardless of the worth of your lover or his potential.

As you read through this book, keep asking yourself what it is you want. Be honest about your answers. Your life will be determined by your desires whether you allow them free expression or not. It doesn't matter if you want a relationship that is completely unconventional or if you're looking for a textbook romance—the best thing you can do for yourself is accept who you are. Only then can you go out and get what you need.

Turning Your Man
Into Putty
in Your Hands

1 | *Relationships*

What Is Love?

Biology and Love

Let's face it—human beings are animals, specifically designed to produce more animals. Millions of years of evolution have brought us to this point, and our needs, desires, and drives have been shaped by these natural forces. Because it takes two to create another human being, most of us are driven to mate. No matter how many times we have been disappointed in love, no matter how much we try to control our impulses, we can't help looking outside of ourselves to fulfill this fundamental part of being human.

Forget the blurring of differences that modern technology has bestowed on us and look at love from a purely biological standpoint. The consequences of "mating" are vastly different for men and women. The female body must carry the child for nine months. The female also plays the largest role in feeding (breast-feeding) and protecting the offspring.

Because the investment is much higher, the majority of females are much choosier than the males when it comes to finding the best mate to produce offspring. Males, on the other hand, usually contribute little more than their semen and can afford to take whatever opportunities happen along. This biological inequality has contributed to the evolution

3

of men and women's different attitudes toward relationships.

Most stereotyped interaction between men and women can be attributed (correctly or not) to this biological directive. Men sleep around because of a drive to distribute their DNA as widely among the population as possible. Women sleep around to insure they get the support and benefits they need—even if it takes many men to provide it for them and their young. Or you could say that men and women chose to be faithful or to marry in order to assure the paternity of the man, who in turn cares for the woman and her young.

So, though the drive to mate exists in everyone, women instinctively are aware that the stakes are much higher for them. What this means is plain: Women take control. Whether it's done overtly or subversively, it does you no good to be a wallflower waiting to get an invitation from a man. It is the woman's place to guide the development of the relationship in the direction she wants it to go. The sooner you stop waiting for a man to do the "right" things, the sooner you'll get the relationship you want.

Society and Love

Why is it that women, most of whom have so much to lose, tend to default to the passive role? Why do men tend to define themselves by their work and accomplishments, while women often make the mistake of defining themselves by their relationships?

Society determines what is currently considered "proper" in fulfilling our biological imperatives. Our culture then trains children to fulfill their expected roles. So on top of the instinctive impulses we all possess, there is the conditioning we receive growing up which is designed to be self-perpetuating.

The ideal of the male/female relationship is based on

"woman as chattel," concept originating in early Western culture. Males had the strength to protect their mates and young, and in exchange, women were forced to submit to men's idea of what a woman should be. That meant a woman had to please her man or be abandoned to the mercy of a violent world. She also had to conform to male-dominated society's ideal of womanhood and suffered ostracism if she transgressed those moral laws. Even today, everything from fairy tales to clichés like "boys will be boys" condition women to expect a more subservient, protected position in their relationships.

It's true that in the postindustrialized world, where laws control violence and strength is no longer the sole barrier between life and death, women have gained a new independence. The women's movement questioned the very foundations of male hierarchy, and sexual freedom was part of the key to achieving equality of the sexes.

By understanding the affect society has had on your development, you can determine if what you feel is a true desire or if it is part of the conditioning you received while growing up. You'll also be able to recognize behavior in your lover that may simply be a conditioned response rather than a reflection of his character. You'll find this conditioning in everything from your ideas of love, marriage, and romance to what stimulates you sexually.

For example, women are conditioned to equate love with being desired. In media and advertising, women are most often depicted from a male point of view, as something to be sought after and claimed. Girls grow up surrounded by desirable images of women, and they soon learn that they are loved when someone "wants" them. It is only recently that a corresponding quantity of male sexual images has arisen, giving young girls their own icons of desire.

This conditioning leads women to become sexually aroused by their lover's desire, while men become aroused over the woman herself. That sets up a complex set of reactions that must interlock perfectly to work. A woman's desirability ultimately rests on her confidence, yet how can she be sure of herself when she places self-validation in another person's hands?

It's not easy to loosen the hold that early training places on people, but through nonaggressive questions and discussion, you can uncover the origins of your behavior in cultural rules. Then you can decide if such thinking is beneficial to you and your lover.

Ultimately, the freer you are of unspoken constraints, the more powerful you will be. Your true desires, not other's opinions, will be the only dictates of your actions.

Women and Love

Perhaps women are will more cautious about sexual expression simply because, for thousands of years, women used sex as the means of getting a commitment from a man. Instincts die hard. A woman wants continued confirmation of her man's commitment, usually in the form of attention, conversation, and declarations like, "I love you." Even a wife, who has received what could be considered the ultimate commitment, in the form of marriage, requires periodic confirmation.

For most women, if they don't receive the cues they expect, they tend to start resenting their lover for not fulfilling the contract he originally agreed to. The trouble is, the most important aspects of the commitment are usually unspoken. What is "love?" If a man says, "I love you," then he does in his own way. But what does being loved mean to you? What does it mean to him? Probably many different things. In today's confusing world, who's to say what love is?

That's the most important thing to remember about love and relationships—the variations are endless. It's inevitable that some men simply don't want to or won't be able to give you what you want. Even if you are compatible, you and your lover aren't likely to have exactly the same ideas of what is included in "love," and that can lead to fundamental rifts. It's up to you to listen to him objectively. Do you want similar things from life and love? Only if both of you do will you be able to make sure your needs are fulfilled.

No lawyer would leave the wording of a contract as vague as most people do with the word "love." If you clearly state your feelings and desires right from the beginning of your interaction, and then support your words by your actions, you'll spend a lot less time and agony on men who aren't what you want and who will never be able to give you what you want.

Independence

The Question of Control

It's not likely that you'll be in control of every situation that comes along, but you are in control of your own life. Even when you give up your control to a man, ultimately, it is your decision to do so.

Sometimes women give up control because it feels safer. The illusion of being safe implies stasis and stability. But you have to keep moving forward for both you and your relationship to grow. Feeling safe will never get *you* where you want to go.

The Chameleon Syndrome
Often, when a woman is in love, she tries to be whatever her lover wants. She mistakenly believes that the way to please a man is to mold herself into his "dream girl." When you find yourself willing to change your looks, the way you dress, your behavior, even your values, then you have a problem on your hands.

Never, ever give up your own dreams or sublimate your

desires for a man. Taking up tennis so you can play every weekend with your boyfriend, or starting to jog with him every morning, may seem like a way to strengthen the relationship even if you aren't that interested in those activities. But that is the very thing that will cause the destruction of the relationship. It may seem like there's peace and harmony for a while, and you are doing things together—but you're living his life. You're creating an illusion of a relationship rather than building a foundation between two real people. Illusions never survive the test of time, and in the end you'll be more disappointed and frustrated than if you'd kept hold of your own likes and desires, and made it clear that you were going to get what you needed from your relationship.

One seemingly innocent way women sublimate themselves to their lovers is by giving up the interests and hobbies that aren't important to him. Often, you don't even realize what you're doing. You may believe you've simply grown out of that phase of bowling or dancing every Saturday night. Or you don't want to take time away from your lover. Yet making a sacrifice of your outside life to the relationship puts pressure on your lover to fulfill every one of your needs. No man can do that.

This desire to change in order to please your lover is an insidious thing. It feels like the *right* thing to do for a man you love. After all, you want *him* to give *you* the things you want. But therein lies the difference. You can't expect him to change what he is, only how he treats you and the relationship. When you jettison aspects of yourself, you are sabotaging the relationship.

Always remember, your lover was attracted to the woman you were, not the woman you try to become for him.

Control Your Own Reactions
If you don't control something, then you have two choices: Get away from it or change your attitude about it.

You are capable of controlling the way you respond to things. Feel secure, confident, and positive, even if you have to fake it. Does that sound dishonest? It's an attitude adjustment. If you smile, it triggers an emotional reflex making you feel happier. If you believe you're confident, if you hold your shoulders straight and look people in the eye, then you will be more confident. Approach situations from a positive point of view and you'll be able to accomplish greater things.

The easiest way to control your reactions is to focus on your priorities. You constantly need to rethink habits and ask yourself why you feel the way you do. The goal isn't to be perfect but to keep other people from deciding where you will go with your life.

This includes your lover. Just because he wants something from you or withholds something from you, your best choice is to *act*; not react. Don't simply respond to his behavior—do what it is you want. Ask for what you want. Don't rest your peace of mind on his compliance. If he is unable to give you what you need, then it's up to you to decide when it's time to find a man who will.

Create Your Own Goals

The only way to make sure you are becoming the person you want to be is to rise above everyday tasks and routines, and see your life in the future. Envision what you want from your life and work toward it. Be the type of person you want to be in your future. That's the way to accomplish anything, be it successful relationship or a successful career.

Remember, people don't change, but they do "transform." That implies a gradual shifting rather than an about-face. Even when we recognize behavior that we'd like to alter, it's not always that easy. Habit goes far deeper than we can consciously trace. That's why it takes constant reevaluation of your priorities and progress to keep yourself in control and on track with your life.

Self-Esteem

Don't ever allow yourself to feel less worthy or belittled by your lover. That doesn't mean fighting with him over comments he makes that can be interpreted as condescending—don't even get that far. You are free to tell him how his statement sounded to you, but never try to make him validate you. Very likely it was an innocent, misinterpreted remark that he is confused about as well.

However, if you repeatedly feel put down and your lover defends his statements and opinion about you, then for some intangible reason he really believes that he is more important than you.

Your only recourse with a man like that is to leave. The only way he'll learn to respect and value you is if you respect and value yourself. You can't do that in his company.

Maintain Other Friendships

It's very important that your lover doesn't become the sole outlet for your deepest feelings. We all hear, "He's my best friend." Fine, but you'd better have other best friends that you can talk to openly and honestly to create balance in your life. If he's the only one you can really talk to, that puts undue pressure on the relationship. Any time you and he have a disagreement, you'll have no one else to talk to about it. The relationship will only be helped if you have other outlets.

Don't Interfere With His Friendships

Just as you need friends as emotional outlets, don't try to alienate your lover from the people he's close to. Your best bet is to discover qualities in his friends and family that you can relate to. Make them your allies. That doesn't mean you have to be bosom buddies, but at the very least be friendly and cooperative.

Being angry about other people he knows or likes gives

them power in your relationship. This includes old girlfriends. It doesn't matter what they did together, how much time they were together, or even how much he loved her. It's the past, and it will only have a bearing on you and your relationship if you allow it to. Fighting about it and spending time on it makes it important, and that's the quickest way to convince *him* that she's still important.

Keep Some Perspective

When you're upset over your relationship and you can't seem to do anything but obsess about what's lacking and what you want, ask yourself, "How will this situation affect my life five years from now?" At the risk of trivializing real emotions, take a cold hard look at what you're feeling. Are you in love with the man or the idea of a relationship with the man? If it's the relationship, then nothing's lost by leaving but a man who wasn't right for you anyway.

If you can't be convinced so easily, consider this: If you're like most people, you probably don't think a lot about past relationships, even if they were very, very important at one time in your life. Even if you had a lover who broke your heart, you only think about him once in a while without feeling too much pain. You eventually get over things like that. You may retain some negative habits that got you into that sort of relationship in the first place, or you may have formed blocks to keep that particular situation from happening again, but the lover himself is no longer important.

Other Options

Don't let yourself get into a situation where you feel you have to stay for lack of any other choice. The more options you have, the more control you have. This doesn't necessarily mean keeping more than one lover just in case one doesn't work out, but arrange your life so that there are other possibilities you can turn to if you need them. This includes maintaining friendships with men and being open to meeting new men.

Nothing is more frustrating than staying in a relationship because you feel you have no other option. Or feeling like the current situation is better than any alternative. That isn't true. You have the capability of making alternatives whatever you want them to be. It may take time and effort, but you can shape your own life as long as you know what you want and don't compromise those desires.

When you're stuck in a frustrating or dangerous situation, don't blame it on your lover or your economic situation. You're in that situation because you're putting yourself there. Apparently, you've taken what you've got and have decided that this is better than being on your own.

But if that's true, you still know the relationship isn't giving you what you want. So don't let an unsatisfactory lover limit your chances of finding someone who will satisfy you. If your relationship isn't fulfilling, what's the worst that could happen from stating what it is you want or allowing yourself to date other men? If your lover leaves because of that, well, you may not like being alone, but no one has ever died from it. At the very least, you'll be completely available for something new, something that will surely satisfy you more than your last relationship.

It's always up to you to go out and create opportunities for yourself. Don't just wait around for something to happen. Get out and meet people, do social things such as taking classes, taking up a sport, going to the theater, attending concerts of meeting friends at nightclubs. Nurture your independence even when you have a lover. Being a confident, independent woman will always get you what you want.

What Do You Want?

To have a successful relationship, you must know what you want. Be honest with yourself. What's important to you?

What will make you happy? Be specific. All women want a loving, sensitive man; but every woman has certain special things that define love to her.

Do you want your lover to make you feel attractive, or exciting, or appreciated? Do you want to be supported financially? Do you want him to do the housework? Do you want a man who is a leader, or do you want a man who does what you want? Do you want him to want a family? Do you want him to be shy or outgoing? And if you want to get married, what exactly does that mean to you?

Take a good long look at those desires you've labeled "marriage" and "love." These are two very abstract concepts. It's important that you analyze what it is you want. That's the only way you'll get it.

Also, examine your old relationships and look for patterns. Which ones had the greatest effect on you, either good or bad? What were you looking for then, and what are you looking for now? How does that make the men you date now different from those you used to date? Where will you be in three years, or five years, or ten years? What sort of man do you envision there with you?

Taking control of your relationships doesn't mean that you're always the one who initiates sex or communication or activities together. Taking control means getting what you want from a man. If the man you're with can't give you those things, then taking control means having the strength to let go and find a man who can and will.

Don't ever be intimidated about going after what you want.

Expectations
If you invest a lot of time deciding what you want from a relationship, it's inevitable that you'll have a mental picture of the actions you expect from your lover. However, while you have the freedom to want the sort of love you want, you

can't demand that type of love from anyone, be it a date, a lover, or your mate.

Objectively consider the man you are with, what he offers you and how you feel about him. Does your lover have the basic qualities you want in a man? Or are you excited by the thought of how he will eventually act as your relationship develops and your love grows?

This is a very important distinction to make. You cannot base your love on future expectations. Yes, you must have your own personal goals for the future. Yes, you must know what you want from a man. But you must be getting what you want from your lover *now*. If you aren't, if you're waiting for that magic moment when he will eventually commit, or care, or talk, or act the way you've always dreamed, then you've living in an illusion.

This search for love becomes a never-ending casting call, as you try to fit whatever man you're dating into your "dream lover" role. Your ideal relationship becomes more complex and impossible to fulfill as time goes by. Failed relationships just intensify the desire to have exactly the kind of love that you've always wanted.

Forget About His Potential

Fall in love with the man, not his potential. Loving what you think he's going to become is impractical. Odds are you don't *know* what he'll be in the future. At the very least, you've got a long wait ahead of you until your man becomes the man you really want.

It's common to find a lover who needs help in one area of his life or another. You commit yourself to solving the problem and helping your lover overcome the things that are keeping him from fulfilling his potential. This sort of relationship fulfills the nurturing impulse as well as the desire to be needed, but it isn't the relationship you want.

Many women seek out men who hold back from them in

some way or another. They believe that by giving enough love and commitment, they can get that love they see right below the surface. They go on quest for a man's love, focusing more time and effort on his needs than on their own careers and interests.

Your primary duty is to develop your own potential, not your lover's, not your mate's. If you don't tend to your own needs, no one else will. After all, you want to be in a caring relationship in which your man loves you, not what you can do for him. The only way to have a healthy relationship is if you love the man for who he is right now, not for what he will be or could be.

Free Yourself of Illusions

You must be objective about what your man is like, not what you want him to be like. Romance is nine-tenths illusion and one part reality. But the worst thing you can do is to make a commitment based on a romantic illusion. You must be able to take off the rose-colored glasses and recognize how your needs in a relationship compares to what this man is capable of giving you.

Discuss the type of relationship you want with your lover. Don't try to fit your goals into something that you think he wants. If you're not honest about your desires, the relationship is doomed. Ask him what he has in mind for a relationship and really listen to what he's saying.

If there are particular needs that aren't being met, then tell your lover specifically what they are. If he wants to give that to you, then great. If he doesn't want to give you what you ask for, even though he says he loves you, you don't have the right to be angry with him. It's his choice what he does with his life, just as you control your own decisions.

You'll need to discuss your desire fully to make sure you are understood. Listen to what he thinks you are asking for. Find out what it means to him. Of course, he may not even know why he feels the way he does, and he has that freedom, too. You can't force him to talk about certain things, but you can try to help him discover what it is he's feeling if you do it in a kind and giving way. Because when your lover is fulfilled, he's more likely to give you what you're asking for in return.

If your lover is unwilling or incapable of doing the things you feel are necessary for the relationship to be a healthy one, then you need to move on. No amount of control on your part can affect basic incompatibility. If you don't have what you want, you're not going to be happy. And your lover has to give you what you want—trying to get the desired behavior out of him by arguing never works.

Love 'em or Leave 'em

You have two choices in a relationship. Be happy with your lover, faults and all; or leave, so you can find one who can give you what you want.

Love 'em. Respect what your lover is capable of giving you. We all have our faults and insecurities. You want a man who loves and accepts you, so you, in return, must accept what he is. Even though you and your lover might not have exactly the same ideas of what is included in your definition of love, if caring and respect and the basic qualities you need in a man are there, then you can always work out compromises as new situations and personal differences come up.

Once you start expecting your lover to fulfill every requirement you have of the "perfect mate," you risk destroying a good relationship. No man will be able to be everything you want.

Leave 'em. Expectations can cause you to sustain relationships that don't satisfy you, in the hope that someday they will. Usually this leads to long, tedious fights about the nature of the relationship. It's easy to get caught up in the vicious cycle of trying to force desired behavior out of your lover when he doesn't give it to you. It goes like this: You fight about it, form an uneasy truce, and when he again falls short, you begin the whole cycle again.

Keep in mind that the majority of relationships end; chances are, either you or your lover will realize that this isn't the love you want. With half of all marriages ending in divorce and the failure rate of less serious relationships much higher than that, it's more than likely that you won't be with your lover forever.

So take some risks. You may get what you want from your current lover if you make it clear that having the opportunity for a relationship that gives you what you want is more important than staying in one that doesn't. If he knows, but doesn't give you, what you need—if you feel an intangible resentment is settling around you like a wet blanket—then it's time for you to leave. You have nothing to lose but a relationship that isn't satisfying you.

Keep Your Distance

We all know what types of men to avoid. We've seen them on TV, in books, and in the movies; and we know right from the start which women are setting themselves up for a lot of pain. Does that stop women from falling in love with these types of men? No. So at the risk of being redundant, here's a short list of men to stay away from.

1. Men who are addicted to drugs or alcohol or gambling and don't acknowledge their condition.
2. Men who are bitter or negative.
3. Men who are extremely jealous or dictatorial.
4. Men who want you to initiate and take care of everything.
5. Men who clearly exhibit antisocial behavior.

These are men who need to solve problems in their own lives. They can't be devoting the time and attention to the relationship that you deserve. You only hurt yourself by devoting your time and attention to their needs rather than your own.

Monogamy

The commitment of marriage is a tricky one to decipher, what with the unspoken guarantees and constraints in the minds of both parties. You may think that by marrying or agreeing to be monogamous you'll automatically get what you want. But that's not necessarily so. The commitment itself is nothing unless your specific needs are being met right *now*, and the goals and values are compatible.

To say that women want a commitment more than men do is incorrect. Everyone has a desire to mate, to one degree or another. Sometimes, this desire is so strong that a person chooses to compromise for the sake of making a commitment. But this leads to disaster. Whenever true desires are compromised, a relationship can't survive for long.

Don't ever make a monogamous commitment based on what you're hoping your lover will give to you or what you expect he will become. That's a trap that will keep you in an unsatisfying relationship, leaving you without the leverage you need to create a relationship that does give you what you want.

Wives
Most women are eager to find and maintain a monogamous relationship. Yet statistics show that the rate of depression is 20 percent higher among married women than single women, while married men are the happiest of all. Obviously, expectations are not being fulfilled for a lot of women.

Just look at the institution of marriage. Women are expected to care for children, husband, and home. Women will do more of the housework and spend more time with the children than their husbands do, even when both partners are working. Women are also traditionally seen as the nurturers, receiving their pleasure from satisfying other's needs.

Women inevitably have their own ideal of what marriage is, and as wives, they try to fulfill that ideal. Do you find yourself doing things your husband prefers, dressing the way he prefers, acting the way he prefers? That's because you're expected to satisfy and please your husband. Yet that often means turning yourself into someone you aren't. The desire to make the marriage a success is often the very thing that puts the most pressure on the wife, eventually killing the sex, the love, and the marriage.

Husbands

Men need women just as much as women need men. According to current surveys, 94 percent of all men marry, and they remarry much more quickly than women after being divorced or widowed. Men live longer when they're married. Not only are divorced men much more likely to commit suicide, but widowers are much more likely to die within six months of their spouse's death than widows are.

Perhaps men in our society thrive better when mated because they expect to be taken care of by their nurturing wife, both emotionally and physically. Traditionally, the wife makes a home for her husband, cares for his injuries, admires him, and eventually gives him children. She also celebrates his successes and comforts him in his failures. She creates an atmosphere of comfort and respect which encourages her husband to be faithful and supportive of her. Wives often take on the burden of communication, watching their husbands carefully to determine what the husband wants and needs without him having to say it.

That may or may not be your idea of a marriage. Is it his? You both may find yourselves trying to fulfill the traditional roles without really examining what it is you want from your marriage.

What Do Men Want?

You love him so you want him to feel good. When you encourage your lover and deal gently with his faults, he'll feel good when he's around you. For many men, that's the definition of love. And the way to keep a man in love with you is by making him feel better when he's with you than when he is with anyone else. That's the way to get what you really want.

Praise Him

The "Alpha-male" theory holds that a female is more attracted to the successful male because he shows he is better able to protect and provide for her and her young. The Alpha-male supposedly also possesses the most desirable qualities to pass on to the next generation.

When you praise and admire your lover, you're doing more than just stroking his ego; you could be fulfilling his biological drive to be a desirable male.

Besides, if you let him know that you think he's great, it's human nature to try to become that. His ego will push him to meet the challenge. That doesn't mean you make yourself a slave to his desires or put yourself down to make him feel more important. Your opinion will be taken much more seriously if your lover sees you as a strong and confident individual.

As far as sexual encounters go, men can be stimulated by praise and admiration in the same way women get pleasure from romance. It's an expression of desire that can help create magic between two people.

Nurture Him

Nurture your lover not only in a physical, caring way, but emotionally as well. We're all looking for helpmates, someone who will help us face life's big challenges, and also with the smaller things, like choosing a good haircut or picking out clothes. If your attitude toward your lover is nurturing and noncritical, he'll be much quicker to listen to your suggestions.

Everyone has insecurities. At one time or another, we've all been a child hurting from something we didn't understand. Recognize the hurt child in everyone. No matter how confident someone might seem, everyone wants confirmation of their worth. Often the more confident a person appears to be, the less confident he actually is.

It's easy enough to find out what's important in a man's life. Listen carefully to what he says. If you can point out the good in something he is uncomfortable about, you've gone a long way to making him feel more secure when he's with you.

Desire Him

Everyone wants a lover who is able to stimulate and satisfy their sexual drive. Since our sexuality is such a powerful force in the development of our characters, its importance to your relationship is undeniable. Almost one half of this book is an examination of different expressions of sexuality and desire, as well as exchanges of power.

When you allow yourself to express your desire freely for your lover, he will be more likely to share his sexuality with you. That way, you can discover the ways your lover becomes sexually excited, while exploring your own sexuality with him. Then your relationship will rest on a strong foundation of intimacy and trust.

Forgive Him

The more serious the relationship, the more likely one or both lovers will sustain negative feelings after a disagreement or miscommunication. Everyone has a unique way of getting over a hurt, but it's inevitable that the deeper the intimacy, the more likely the hurt will be serious.

Feeling anger is part of being human, and suppressing your anger can be dangerous to your health. Yet anger in and of itself doesn't accomplish anything when it is directed toward someone you love. You have to get past the anger to resolve an issue, and the best way to approach a problem between two people is in a supportive, nonjudgmental way.

How do you get your lover to respond to you this way? By approaching him with a caring, forgiving attitude when something does go wrong. Don't indulge in blame or vent your feelings on him. The fact that your lover has hurt you does not give you justification to hurt him back. Contrary to our instinctive "fight back" response, this doesn't balance the scale or do the relationship any good.

Always acknowledge the commitment you've made before examining what is bothering you. That will place your mutual goals squarely in front of you both before anything else is said. It needn't be presented as a challenge, either. Assume that your commitment still holds and that the love you share puts you and your lover on the same side. If you work from a position as allies, you'll be able to sort out any miscommunication that might occur.

Listen to Him

The only way you get to know someone is by listening. That seems to go without saying, doesn't it? But often when you're drawn to someone with whom you feel a rapport, your urge is to tell them everything about your own dreams and plans. It's very easy to fall into an illusion about a man or a relationship if you're the only one building it. Don't let your impulse to create intimacy interfere with the natural growth and development of the relationship.

It is counterproductive to open yourself too much, too quickly, to anyone. You want to give people a chance to want to know you. The more a man wants to know you, the more important any of your thoughts and feelings will be to him. Aside from what he wants, that's what *you* really want him to give you, isn't it?

Keys to a Good Relationship

Support the Relationship
Don't put the relationship on the line when you argue. That sounds like a contradiction, doesn't it? If you don't get what you want, there's a good chance you'll leave, right? So why not make that threat?

Well, the only chance you have to find a way through the problems in the relationship is to work together. Neither of you is going to be able to do it on your own. You have to cooperate for communication to take place. If the relationship is put under question along with every disagreement, it's only a matter of time before it is over.

Keep in mind that the person who constantly calls the state of the relationship into question is the one giving up control. Every time that threat is used, it carries less weight until it means nothing at all. The last thing you want is the status of your relationship to be unimportant.

Right and Wrong
To create a good relationship, you must have an atmosphere that is noncritical. That's the only way you'll be able to explore new paths that open up, whether it's sexual

expression or who cleans the kitchen. Once you start judging behavior as good or bad, you start placing false limits on each other's responses.

It might sound strange, but you are never wrong. You always do what's right for you. To say that you're wrong means someone other than you is interpreting and judging your choices.

Conversely, other people are never wrong for themselves, either. You can't pass judgment—only observe and see patterns. After all, you'll never really know why someone has chosen to do something. By keeping this concept in mind, communication will open up between you.

This means that day-to-day irritations, which are usually symptoms of other problems, will be dealt with in a way that won't bog you down in petty details. For example, you may argue over the fact that he wants to watch television while you want to go out to dinner. Neither choice is right or wrong, even if your lover has done nothing but watch television for the past week. If you accept that he does what he needs to do, he will be much more open to accepting your feelings and desires. When you both know there is no need to go on the defensive, you'll feel comfortable enough to discuss why you want to do what you do. Then you can work out a compromise wherein both of you can get what you need.

Arguments

Arguments are usually misunderstandings, not disagreements. Misunderstandings are usually communication problems, while disagreements are fundamental differences in attitudes and values.

We each attach different nuances and meanings to words. Personality, background, and conditioned expectations contribute to the definitions of these words. Which constitutes reality, his opinion or yours? Our assumptions color our responses more than the reality of the situation. Most arguments classically begin when one person gets angry and the other one isn't even aware of it having done something wrong. That's almost always a simple-definition problem.

Conflicts exist in our most fundamental opinions about ourselves—you feel you're worthy because you got good grades in college and have a good job, but you're unworthy because you're fifteen pounds overweight and don't have a man in your life. With internal contradictions like that, it's natural for misunderstandings to emerge between two people

Both of you owe it to each other to try to see the other's point of view. Truly try. Remember, he isn't wrong, He's doing what is very right for him at this time. Being defensive or angry keeps you from understanding his motivations. After all, if you've agreed that you want a relationship with each other, neither one of you intends to do things purposely that will upset or drive the other away. If you start from this point, you'll be able to get much closer to understanding him and communicating your own feelings.

Get Rid of "Should"

When you say "should," you are glossing over the real reason you want to do or have something. Assumptions must be questioned in order to find the truth. Your lover should respect you. Why? Because you want to be considered equal? Or are you waiting for him to acknowledge you as his equal, instead of claiming that status on your own? It's very important to understand your feelings on this. "Should's" often indicate areas in which you rest your opinion on someone else's.

Arguing over "should's" can be dangerously superficial and slippery. Stop yourself when you hear the word. Probe deeper to find out what you really feel about the situation.

This will deepen the communication between you. It's the same sort of idea as eliminating the categories of "right" and "wrong." You're able to get to the heart of matters when you stop trying to place blame or impose limits.

Also, when you hear someone tell you that you should do something, ask them why. You'll find out more about a person's beliefs by examining his "should's" than anything else.

Jealousy

You feel jealous when you allow someone else to control your reaction to your lover. Other people have nothing to do with your relationship. Not his old girlfriends or ex-wife, not his mother, or your mother, of your friends...When you're both discussing what you want, don't involve other people's expectations or desires. Only yours and his matter. Even if you don't believe that, pretend. It never hurts to ignore jealous feelings, and with practice, it can improve your life never to let other people's opinions affect your emotional equilibrium.

It is best in the long run not to delve into the sexual particulars about former lovers. Whatever you do, don't compare your lover's behavior in bed to anyone else's, even if he comes out ahead. No one appreciates being judged, and if you criticize your old lover, your current lover may wonder what you're not saying about him.

Women Watching

Admire other women when your lover does, and point it out to him when women compliment or look at him. Does it sound crazy? Well, you'll never stop him from looking at other women by disliking it.

Our society says that men are more visually attuned while women respond better to verbal signals. But there's nothing physiological about this response—it's just one of the ways boys and girls become conditioned as they grow up. By acknowledging that your lover has learned to respond to women by looking at them and accepting his reaction, you are subtly bringing his response into the area in which women hold sway—talking about it. In effect, you are guiding his impulses toward communication, something that will make you more comfortable. After all, it doesn't matter what other women look like, you just want to make sure your lover wants to be with you.

Encouraging him to express his opinions freely puts you in the position of power. You have allowed him to look and watch. You can even bring an attractive woman to his attention yourself. Your lover will feel like he has his cake and can eat it, too. Why would any man want to leave that? In fact, if you can master this simple form of giving, you'll find he is much more open to you, both sexually as well as emotionally. That empowers you in the relationship.

Time Together

Do you have common interests? What exactly are they? Spending time together doesn't mean giving up the things you like to do and taking part in only his favorite activities. If you find yourself doing that, take another look. You might not have as much in common as you think you do.

It's also important to continue doing things together after the first flush of excitement and romance has worn off. Ideally, both of you will discover new things to do together, but take the lead if you must. Don't expect your lover to make sure you are involved in things together, or get upset that he isn't taking the initiative and suggesting new activities. This is one of those cases where you can take control by example and encouragement. So do it. If you truly are compatible, you'll be able to find ways to spend enjoyable time together. That's the only way to keep a relationship vital.

Getting What You Want

What if the man you want doesn't seem interested? Or the man you have is what you want, but he doesn't do everything you'd like him to do?

Compatibility is essential, but you can't expect your lover to *know* what you need. None of us can read minds. You also can't expect your lover to take the initiative on finding out what you need. Your desires are too important for you to be passive about them. Take control. Learn what your lover needs from you, while teaching him what it is you want.

Don't Compromise Your Desires

Particularly in a new relationship, you must be clear about what it is you want. If some behavior or action is essential for your happiness, then don't compromise. For instance, if you don't like last minute get-togethers—perhaps it makes you feel taken for granted—then tell him you won't see him unless you have set a date. Don't give in, because then there's no reason for him to do what you want. And if he doesn't make plans to see you, then you haven't lost anything but a man who isn't treating you the way you want.

If you are firm in the beginning, and there is a true desire on his part to get to know you and please you, then you can get almost anything you want. But remember, though your true desires shouldn't be compromised, occasionally you'll have to compromise on the way your lover gives you what you need. No one will ever have the perfect lover they've imagined for themselves, but you could get something better if you gently and confidently set about getting what you want.

Manipulating

The definition of manipulation is: to handle or manage with skill or dexterity; to control or manage the course of action. Why has manipulation gotten such a bad rap? Because by popular definition manipulation includes unfair or insidious tactics.

Women have been mostly relegated to submissive roles throughout history; as a result, they have resorted to manipulating their lovers to get what they want—i.e., convincing the man that he's getting what he wants, while he's really giving her what she wants. Women usually did this when men held the positions of power.

Now, of course, women are gaining equal access to power. But we are in a period of transition. Many women still find it easier to use manipulation rather than openly and honestly stating what it is they want and compromising only on how they get it.

Manipulation itself is not negative, but refusing to admit that you have manipulated your lover is tantamount to refusing to admit you have equal access to control in your relationship. Admit it to yourself, at least, and realize that you have the power to take overt steps to direct the relationship where you want it to go.

Reverse Psychology

Here's an example of how you can get your lover to do what you want, while he thinks he's getting what he wants.

Reverse psychology can work in almost any situation. If you want him to spend more time with you, but he doesn't ever have the time, then go out on your own. Let him know how much fun you're having and all the interesting people you're meeting. Be nonchalant, even a little hesitant, about having him join you. When you notice that his interest is warming, then it's time to have a discussion. He's interested enough to listen to your side now, and with a little encouragement, there's nothing you can do to stop him joining you.

People want what they think they can't have. Particularly in the beginning of a relationship, it can heat someone's interest even faster if you're not always available. Everyone knows how unattractive desperate people are—and even the smallest taint of desperation can turn your lover off.

Getting an "Uninterested" Man

What if you meet a man you like, but he doesn't seem interested? The worst thing you can do is seem very interested in him right away. Men don't respond to being desired in the same way women do. Most women equate attention with love, but for many men attention from a woman just feeds the ego. If you are giving him all that attention, why should he make any additional effort to give you what you want?

So, when you meet a man who doesn't pursue a relationship with you even though you've dropped a few hints:

- Put yourself in a position to find out if he is willing to be your friend. If he likes you enough to want to talk to you and have you around, then you have an open door to pursue a relationship with him.
- Put aside your desire to have an intimate relationship with him. You aren't having one, and it can only develop slowly. There's nothing men hate worse than having a woman they haven't even had two thoughts about becoming dependent on them. Your confidence and commitment to your own goals will keep pressure from falling on him.
- Talk about him and find out his insecurities. Make him comfortable with you and happy when you're around. This is the time to find out if you really do like this person. Are these the qualities and character that you want? Or is it only "the relationship" you want, and you think you can cast this man in the role of the hero?

- When he does begin to show interest in your life, don't snatch at it like it's a life preserver. Accept it as your natural due. What you're trying to do is to create a habit of him wanting *you*. You already know you want him.
- Don't have sex with him as soon as he wants it. You don't want just to have sex, you want to create desire. Once he's starting to like you enough to want to be more intimate with you, a little frustration can go a long, long way.

Being Seductive

Men would rather you approach them as people than immediately try to turn them on. Seductiveness is alluring, but many women make the mistake of always being "on" when a man they're interested in is around. It ends up being fake and superficial. Besides, if you change the way you act when a man is around, then it's the man who has control of the situation. You're just reacting.

Also, don't give way to the challenge of getting a man to desire you. People usually know when they come up short in a manhunt. Effort simply becomes a waste of time that is designed to serve your ego. If the man doesn't respond, you are building habits of behavior between the two of you which will destroy any chance of his wanting you in the future.

The effect of serenely accepting his disinterest while gracefully keeping your distance can do more to draw a man after you than any other trick in the book.

Getting a Commitment

Most people fight against committing to a relationship when it is plain that it's the relationship that's important, not themselves. Whether it's having sex or moving in together, people want to feel they are wanted for themselves, not what they can give their lover. You can give this impression by moving a relationship along faster than your lover is comfortable with.

If your lover is commitment-shy, the simple answer is not to push it. Begging for his love or arguing about behavior will not make your lover desire you. Let your lover know what sort of commitment you want, and let him know you're going to get it. Whether it's from him or another man, it's his choice.

Whatever you do, don't commit to your lover if he hasn't made the commitment you want. You'll never get what you want by giving yourself away carelessly. You have a goal in mind as to what kind of relationship you want, and the only way to make sure you get it is not to settle for less.

2 | *Physical Considerations*

Beauty

Beauty is, for women, the ultimate dilemma. Haven't all women, while growing up, searched their faces in the mirror and wondered: Am I beautiful? Am I ugly? It was one of the unanswerable questions. And how could you trust your mother's judgment that yes, you were indeed beautiful? Especially when your friends seemed to have completely different criteria for beauty. Only one thing was certain— the illusive quality of "beauty" is *very* important for women.

Women grow up thinking beauty is essential to happiness because we're conditioned by fairy tales and love stories to believe that comes with the prince, and love, and happiness-ever-after. Like Sleeping Beauty, we will awaken when our prince arrives. Like Cinderella, we will be relieved of drudgery and sadness by our prince. Like Snow White, we will be saved and protected by our prince. Aside from goodness, the most important criteria for a fairy-tale maiden was beauty.

And now, in our "vogue" society, a woman's image is still of utmost importance. Glossy magazines are filled with close-ups of gorgeous, perfect women, while movies and advertising unite sexual excitement with the concept of beauty. Even self-help and women's magazines are sup-

33

ported by advertisers who make money from making women beautiful—selling makeup, skin care, or clothing. Women are told they need to work harder at being beautiful, and are bombarded with diets, articles on physical self-improvement, how to apply makeup, etiquette, and a long list of do's and don'ts. Men's magazines are only now starting to publish such things. It serves to continue the conditioning that keeps women dependent on outside approval and insecure about validating their own self worth.

Society values beauty, so women place disproportionate value on their physical selves. After all, those women who do fit society's criteria for beauty are often rewarded. The "beautiful" women are sought after, admired, and lifted to the plane of the privileged few.

But that view of beauty is superficial, and any success or achievement on that scale will inevitably not be satisfying. Confidence, not physical appearance, is the real source of beauty. No matter what you look like, you have to love your body and your *self* to be truly beautiful.

And even when your lover does think you're beautiful, it usually isn't enough. That's because women mistake beauty-validation for an affirmation of their self-worth; but confidence must be innate to be real. No man can give worth to a woman, yet women are trained by society to seek it this way.

Men agree. One of the things men dislike the most are women who are overconcerned or insecure about their physical appearance. Many men hate it when a woman fusses with her hair, or moans about her diets, or can't find anything to wear that doesn't make her look awful. Most men don't like to see a lot of makeup on their lover's face, particularly foundation, powder, and blusher. Skin is a turn-on for most men. And heavy lipstick or wet gloss may make you look more dramatic, but you're much less kissable. Men may value beauty in women, but they don't have much patience for the superficiality of the pursuit of beauty.

Men will inevitably accept your attitudes about yourself. If you believe you have a great, sexy body that's just dying for his touch, he'll want to touch you. If you hide your body or are embarrassed about certain aspects of yourself, then it's likely that your lover will believe that, too. And if you're constantly putting yourself down, he'll have a hard time finding a reason to praise you. It doesn't matter if, according to society's standards, you're fifteen or fifty pounds overweight. It doesn't matter if you're eighteen or sixty. If you love yourself, your lover will too.

Know your own body, keep healthy, and feel good about your life. That's the magic combination that makes beauty.

Aging

Aside from the fairly recent discovery and use of certain anti-aging creams like Retin-A there is very little you can do to prevent or retard the effects of aging. Surgery can stretch skin, but it can't repair it; Collagen can "plump up" the lines around your eyes but it can't make them disappear.

As Naomi Wolf in her book *The Beauty Myth* states, "For twenty years the holy oils made 'scientific' claims, using bogus charts and figures, of 'proven improvement' and 'visible difference' that were subject to no outside verification.... There has been no public move to put pressure on the cosmetic industry to print retractions or apologies to women; nor in the coverage of the change in FDA regulations has the possibility been raised of financial compensation for the women consumers cheated so thoroughly for so many years."

Since 1987, when such claims became illegal to make, advertisers have continued to play on consumer fears by failing to retract the unspoken assumption—established by decades of earlier advertisements—that antiaging products do work unconditionally.

The only healthy way to deal with aging is to accept it and revel in it. Let's be realistic—we may spend time minutely examining our own faces, but who else cares or notices the things you do? The fact is, faces become more interesting as they age, because people gain experience and confidence with age. But you must believe that, otherwise you'll never be able to accept how you look and who you are.

The Female Body

If you don't know every nook and cranny of your body, how will your lover know? It's up to you to reveal yourself to him and invite him to explore your entire body—not just the sex organs, but every tender, ticklish, thrilling part.

Whoever came up with the idea that "mystery" was sexy may well have been off the mark. In the case of the human body, the more intimately and thoroughly you know both your own body as well as your lover's, the more thoroughly you will be satisfied in your sexual encounters.

Skin
Your skin covers your entire body, and it serves as the conduit of one of your five senses—tactile sensation. Your skin can be stimulated in thousands of pleasurable ways. Skin also exudes human odor, a fact that is extremely underappreciated in our sanitized society.

If you want your body worshipped, then explore and savor every part of your lover's body. This is another instance where showing by example works; but it also helps to ask. Tell him how good it feels to touch him, and tell him how good it would feel if he returned the compliment.

Sex Organs
Get a mirror and examine yourself. Don't do it just once; you owe it to yourself to really get to know your own body and its responses. It may be slightly uncomfortable for

women to see their own sex organs, but it's not impossible. How else can you love your body if you aren't familiar with it?

The Vulva. The vulva is the part of a woman's sex organs that can be seen: the mons veneris (Mound of Venus), the outer lips (labia majora) and inner lips (labia minora), the vaginal opening, the urethra, and the clitoris.

The mons veneris is the padding of flesh over the pubic bone. It is covered by strands of pubic hair. The mons is remarkably responsive to stroking and pressure.

The outer lips protect everything else. In some women, these folds of flesh are thick and meet over her sex organ. In others, the lips are mere fleshy bumps that lie to either side of the sex organs. Each woman is different, just as each man's penis is different.

The inner lips are very tender and delicate. During arousal, they are usually moistened by vaginal lubricant.

The urethra is positioned within the inner lips, just below the clitoris and above the entrance to the vagina. Don't ever insert anything into the urethra. This area is very sensitive, and it is an entirely personal thing whether it is pleasurable for your urethra to be touched.

The Clitoris. The small hood that forms at the joining of the inner lips protects the clitoris. Only the tip of the clitoris can be seen, like a tiny pink pea. When a woman is aroused, the clitoris fills with blood just like a man's penis, pushing it slightly out of the protective hood.

It is the stimulation of the clitoris that leads to female climax. The action of a man's penis entering the vagina tugs on the inner lips, pulling the hood against the clitoris. The man's pubic bond rubbing against the clitoris also causes arousal.

Something this important should be shown to your lover. There is simply no excuse for letting him fumble around your crotch looking for your clitoris. Show him what it looks like and how you touch yourself to become aroused. Tell him how it feels when he touches you there.

The Vagina. It's a mistake to think of the vagina as a hole. The vagina is a hollow ring of muscles, approximately four inches long.

The upper and lower ends of the vagina are the narrowest. The opening of the vagina is partially covered by the labia minora, the inner lips, which become engorged with blood during intercourse. In most virgins the actual opening of the vagina is partially closed by a thin fold of tissue known as the hymen.

Nowadays, the hymen is often broken when a girl first begins to use tampons.

The cervix of the uterus connects to the front of the inner end of the vagina. The cervix is a firm, mushroom shaped bump. The small dent in the center is an opening that leads to the uterus, where a woman is impregnated. Diaphragms and sponges are used to cover the cervix. IUD's are inserted through the opening of the cervix into the uterus.

There are no glands inside the vagina. The mucus that lubricates the vaginal cavity mostly comes from the uterus through the cervix. However, the cells in the lining produce a limited amount of lactic acid, which nurtures sperm as they make their way to the uterus.

When a woman climaxes, she does not ejaculate in the same way a man does. As her arousal increases, the flow of lubricating fluid increases. During climax, the muscles of the inner walls of the vagina ripple and contract, the intensity depending on the strength of these muscles. This pushes lubricant out of the vagina, sometimes creating the appearance of ejaculation.

You can bring yourself to arousal by clenching and releasing the muscles in your vagina. These are the same muscles that you use to stop urinating. Try it. It's an easy, inconspicuous way to give yourself a little thrill.

Breasts

Almost every woman has some reservation about the beauty of her breasts. They are too small, too big, too droopy...But they are perfect for you.

Never ever let a man's opinion prompt you to enlarge or reduce the size of your breasts. He could walk out of your life tomorrow, but your breasts will always be with you.

Menstruation

There is no medical reason why you shouldn't have intercourse while you're menstruating. The menstrual flow is not pure blood, but is a blood-rich lining that mixes with the normal lubricant fluids present in the vagina.

Some women actually feel more excited at this time of the month. Indeed, the muscle contractions during intercourse and climax can ease cramping. If you accept menstruation as a normal body function that isn't to be shunned or ignored, your lover will too.

The Male Body

Knowledge is power. Explore your lover's body both lovingly and thoroughly. Discovering his physical responses will reveal other paths of his sexuality that you can pursue together.

For example, spend one sexual encounter exploring his feet. Massage him, stroke him, tickle him, scratch his sole's with your fingernails. Make it an entire sensual experience. Another time, wash his hair for him, or take a shower with him, rubbing every part of his body with a soft sponge. Don't expect reciprocation in every encounter. If you give him treats this sensual, it won't take much hinting before he's returning the favor and rubbing your feet for you or asking you to take baths with him.

If you really want to turn your man into putty in your

hands, the best place to start is with his body. Examine his body and tell him what you see. Are there any curves or bulges? Fine fuzz or hair? When you point out what might be perceived as flaws, stroking them and teasing him about them, that's the best way to truly capture his attention. Most men will adore the concentrated attention, yet you put yourself in a position of power by judging his physical state.

You have an entire body to play with. Go have fun.

The Penis

A man's sex organs aren't much different from yours. The clitoris and the penis are composed of the same type of sensitive tissue. Your outer lips and his scrotum are also similar. Your lover's genitals aren't foreign territory, but something you already know a lot about.

Basically the penis is a shaft of spongy tissue that fills up with blood when a man is sexually aroused. The plumlike head of the penis or glans is particularly full of hypersensitive nerve endings.

At one time or another, all men have worried about their penis. Their concerns range from its size and shape to the quality and duration of their erection. Be kind and gentle. Just as women tend to link their sexual desirability with how attractive they are, a man often hangs his masculinity on his penis.

It's a tricky psychological balancing trick, because a man's erection is not solely dependent on the physical mechanisms of his penis—it ultimately rests on his mental and emotional state. The three main erection problems are listed below.

Premature Ejaculation

There is no time limit that defines premature ejaculation. A man prematurely ejaculates if he *usually* climaxes before his lover can have an orgasm.

It's possible that he simply needs more physical contact with you. Give him hugs and massages. Cuddle with him. That way he won't want to climax simply from touching you.

If you're frustrated by the brevity of sex, talk it over with your lover in a completely unemotional way. If you accuse him of not satisfying you, it will just make things worse. One simple solution to suggest is using a condom. The rubber sheath can desensitize his penis.

You can also help him learn to control his climax with manual stimulation. Masturbate him almost to orgasm, then stop and stroke his chest or legs until he's under control, then begin stimulating him again. Don't let him bring himself to orgasm while you're doing this. The start, stop, start, stop rhythm will drive him crazy, but the resulting orgasm will be incredibly intense. He'll love you for it.

Interrupted Intercourse

What do you do if you are making love and suddenly his erection starts to fade? Inevitably, a woman's first thought will be that she's done something wrong or isn't attractive enough. Meanwhile, the man is suffering intense confusion and humiliation. A recipe for disaster.

Don't make a big deal about it. A man's erection is not completely voluntary, and absolutely anything can interfere. And it's not just men this happens to. Many women have experienced a time during sex when they suddenly, inexplicably turn off. It could be an intrusive sound, or a sudden thought, or a painful movement. But women are able to bluff their way through intercourse whereas men cannot.

It could be stress, worry, tension, fatigue, etc. Alcohol, though it may make a man feel amorous, almost always interferes with a firm erection. Narcotics and tranquilizers do the same thing.

If your lover is persistently unable to maintain an erection, he should visit a doctor. There could be a physical reason, and if that's ruled out, then you may need to do some honest talking with him to find out what's behind this.

Impotence

You don't need to be concerned if your lover occasionally suffers from impotence. It's just one of the natural consequences of such a complex act, dependent on both physical and mental factors.

If your lover is often impotent or has interrupted intercourse, he needs to explore the psychological reasons why it's happening.

It could be simple anxiety about something in your sexual life or regarding your relationship. It could be stress, or fatigue, or outside pressures from family or job. It could be rooted in his attitudes about sex. It could be a health problem.

In a caring and nonjudgmental way, you are free to pursue possible reasons for his impotence. Whatever you do, don't drag your own ego into it. Remember, you're an independent, powerful woman. You have control over your life, and this is not a direct reflection on you or your worth.

If you both cover all possibilities, and are honestly at a loss for the reason, then there is still something you can do—a little home sex therapy. You and your lover can agree that there will be no intercourse for four weeks. That has to be the rule, and you both have to stick by it even if he does get a good erection. You should cuddle and fondle one another, and you should include his penis even if it doesn't respond. If he wants to help you reach climax, that's wonderful. Don't hold back from enjoying yourself because you aren't having intercourse.

You'll find there are plenty of fun ways to have sex that doesn't rely on your lover's penis. Usually all it takes for a

man to keep an erection is knowing that everything isn't
dependent on it.

Contraception

Worst case scenario—you get pregnant. Do you really
want to deal with that? If you don't, you better take
responsibility for contraception.

Since women are conditioned to respond to men's desire,
they equate being "swept off their feet" with romance and
love. However, contraception requires forethought. Don't let
society's conditioning draw you into an unwanted pregnancy. You control your own attitude about sex, and you
ought to respect yourself enough to have protected intercourse. A man who thinks less of you for making sure
you're protected is irresponsible and selfish, and is not a
man you want for a lover.

Anyway, in this day of AIDS, you should always have
your lover wear a condom even if you are in a monogamous
relationship unless both you have tested negative. If you are
ever going to make a stand on something, the first place to
start is to make sure you're protected during a deadly
epidemic.

If you are in a monogamous relationship with your
partner, and you both check clean of HIV, then there are
other methods of contraception. Discuss it with your lover.
After all, you engage in the most intimate activity that's
possible between two people. And your choice of contraception will inevitably have an affect on your sexual
encounters.

Condoms
The condom is the contraception of choice in the AIDS
era. Take time to find a brand of condom that you are
comfortable with. Some brands are thinner than others,

some are lubricated with powder or jelly. You can get different colors, different textures, and even different sizes.

One type of condom you should know about is the lamb's skin condom. It is made from a part of lamb's intestine. Lamb's skin condoms can be almost three times as expensive as the latex condoms, but they are natural and *super-sensitive*. But because they are made of natural material, they aren't as effective at stopping the AIDS virus.

The Pill

For many women, the Pill is the preferred method of contraception.

The Pill contains hormones that simulate pregnancy, preventing a woman from ovulating. The negative side effects can include weight gain, tender breasts, headaches, nausea—and so on, down to blood clotting and stroke. There may also be more difficulty producing vaginal lubrication.

The positive side effects can include reduced cramping, reduced menstrual flow, and reduced hormonal fluctuations—better known as PMS (Premenstrual Syndrome).

Since the Pill is a hormone, it directly affects the woman's body. Don't ever be pressured into using the Pill against your better judgment. Your lover may not like condoms, but they can't possibly give him blood clots and strokes.

Diaphragm

This is a stiff rubber ring, anywhere from two to three inches across, with a flexible rubber dome. It fits over the cervix and prevents sperm from entering the uterus. Spermicidal cream is important, because the diaphragm only rests against the cervix; it doesn't form a seal.

Unfortunately, diaphragms have to be inserted just before sex. This means breaking off at the beginning or in the middle of things. From both a hygienic point of view and from the need to use fresh spermicide, it's impossible for you always to wear your diaphragm just to be prepared for sex.

Sponges are used like diaphragms and also have heavy doses of spermicides in them. Sponges have advantages because they can be left in for twenty-four hours, and they feel remarkably like the lining of the vagina.

Cervical caps are simply smaller versions of the diaphragm. It's important that cervical caps are fitted correctly, since they adhere with a sort of suction directly to the cervix. Usually, spermicides aren't used with cervical caps, so they aren't as messy as diaphragms. However, cervical caps are more difficult to insert and remove.

IUD
IUD is short for Intrauterine Device. This method involves inserting a small plastic device into the uterus. It can be, among others, shaped in a coil of a T. It prevents a fertilized egg from embedding in the lining of the uterus.

The problems of IUD's include penetration of the uterus walls and infection caused by the device. And, occasionally, a man's penis comes in contact with the small string attached to the IUD that sticks through the cervix. You'll know it if it happens because he'll scream when the tip of his penis hits the sharp end of the nylon string.

Withdrawal
This is not a recommended method of contraception. Sperm leaks from the penis before a man actually ejaculates. Even the tiniest drop can impregnate a woman.

Also, you'll both be thinking so much about the impending moment of withdrawal that you probably won't be able to fully enjoy the experience. You want to lose yourself when you have intercourse, not have him calculating how much longer he can last.

Rhythm Method

This method involves having sex only on certain days of the month, when the woman is not fertile. Some women use a rather sophisticated combination of temperature readings and observation of the lubricant fluid coming from the cervix. Others simply estimate when their ovulation will occur according to the calendar—*approximately* fourteen days after the start of her last period. Only women who are absolutely regular in their cycle can consider this method.

Statistics show that users of rhythm and withdrawal methods bear more children than users of other types of birth control

AIDS

AIDS affects almost everyone's life in some way. Perhaps you know someone who has AIDS or is infected with HIV. More than likely, you've wondered about your chances of having or getting the virus. The truth is, everyone runs the risk of getting AIDS, and HIV travels the easiest from men to women. It's up to you to protect yourself.

What is AIDS?

AIDS stands for Acquired Immune Deficiency Syndrome. The immune system breaks down and can't protect you against often fatal diseases. AIDS is spread by a virus, HIV (Human Immunodeficiency Virus). HIV is carried in blood and semen and can infect you if it enters your body or blood stream. Someone can carry HIV and not have AIDS or show any signs of being sick. But they can transmit the invisible infection through sex or shared drug paraphernalia.

How Do You Get AIDS?

AIDS is not spread by casual contact. You can't get it from coughing, kissing, hugging, sneezing, sweat, tears, touching doorknobs or toilet seats, dishes or swimming pools, or from sharing cigarettes or joints.

No one has gotten AIDS from living with, touching, or caring for a person with AIDS, even in households with young children.

HIV enters the body through mucous membranes, the walls of the vagina, the lining of the rectum, from abrasions on the inside of your mouth and throat, or through direct contact with the blood stream. The virus can't enter through the skin, unless the skin is broken or cut and another person's infected body fluids enter the blood stream.

You can get HIV from:

1. Semen, vaginal fluids, and menstrual blood.
2. Shooting drugs with shared needles.
3. Transfusions of contaminated blood.

Protect Yourself

Use latex condoms. Make them an integral part of sex and not an embarrassing, fumbling intermission. Eroticize the application of the condom. Anything on earth can be eroticized, so it's not hard to when you're dealing directly with a man's penis. Stroke him as you apply the condom, maintain eye contact, and kiss him before and after.

Also, become knowledgeable about condoms. There are more brands and choices than ever before. With very little effort, you'll be able to find one that works for both of you. Never be shy about buying condoms, either. This is your life we're talking about.

AIDS Testing

There is an antibody test that is used to find the antibodies a person produces when they have been infected with HIV. It's not completely reliable, so false negatives do occur.

A positive test means that you've been infected with HIV and that your body has begun producing these antibodies. It doesn't mean you currently have AIDS, but it is currently believed that the majority of people who are HIV positive will develop AIDS over a period of years. People with HIV have to be particularly careful of their health in order to keep AIDS from developing. Since AIDS doesn't show up right away, it is very important to take the tests periodically especially if you've had many sexual partners.

Call your city Department of Health for information on testing sites. Often, there will be pre- and post-test counseling involved.

3 | *Sexual Encounters*

Romance

Romance tends to be relegated to the preliminary step of a sexual relationship. Once the relationship has been established, the romance often dies away because it's no longer seen as necessary.

But what is romance? For many people, it's the affection and attention, tinged with sexual desire, that has come to symbolize love. Whether it's a certain touch, a look, a desire to share feelings or please a lover in a special way, romance directly supports the emotional side of a sexual relationship.

For many women, if they don't get these cues, resentment can set in. Men, on the other hand, learn to give and receive love in different ways. Many men are more comfortable simply expressing their love through their sexual encounters and by being a presence in their lover's life.

If you want more romance, it's up to you to show your lover how to be romantic with you. The best way to get romance is by freely giving it. Don't resent the fact that you're having to take control in this area, and instead, overtly provide opportunities for romance to flourish. Tell your lover about your fantasies and day dreams, and point out exactly what sort of behavior turns you on. Listen to his ideas of romance and love, and encourage him to explore his

own responses in this area. You can do this in a sexy way—
if you're describing something that truly excites you, it
stands to reason you'll be getting a little thrill just talking
about it.

Staying open to new things will help put romance back
into your life. After all, doing something you wouldn't
normally do is the quickest way to shake up a routine. It
doesn't have to be flamboyant or contrived. Allow your
quirky side free rein. Don't you want him to be interesting,
too? A little fun goes a long way to livening up your
relationship.

This includes being open to new ways of sexual expression. Just because men seem to reject romance in favor of
sex, don't cut off what may be your only path back to
romance and intimacy. Exploring your sexuality is really a
direct path to your subconscious desires. Finding out why a
man responds the way he does to certain sexual cues can
give insight to his emotions, providing you with a clear road
map of his motivations. Understanding will inevitably
deepen your love, and you'll both learn what to do to make
each other happy.

Affection
If you only touch your lover when you want sex, your
relationship won't be affectionate.

Affection is nonsexual intimacy and attention. Like romance, many people equate affection with love. Sometimes,
however, we start to see all physical contact as sexual and
have trouble distinguishing between affection and foreplay.

Respond to your lover's touch, but don't always allow it to
go all the way through to a sexual encounter. There must be
hugs and caresses outside of sex or you'll both be deprived
of the emotional bond that enriches sexual encounters.

You won't get affection by asking for it. You have to give it
to get it. If you aren't interested in stroking his hair or

cuddling together on the couch, he probably won't be either. If you don't want to take the effort to cover his feet with a blanket or do one of his chores when he's tired, he won't do that for you. Even the silly romantic things—gifts, notes, flowers—can affirm your lover's importance. Do the things you would like to receive in return, and be clear about what you want without being demanding.

Also, be attentive to your lover in front of other people. Affirming your bond in public will affect the way your relationship is treated by others.

When you're giving him this sort of treatment, you are fully justified in requesting it in return. Your lover, if he's worth anything, will gladly give what you ask for.

Talking About Sex

The idea of sex as something mysterious and profound is a very compelling one for most people. But catering to the "mood" by avoiding honest discussion does far more harm than good, particularly if you want to have sex with a man more than once.

Most people are shy when talking about sex because it's such an intimate and personal response. But there's no way of knowing if you're fulfilling your lover's needs unless you talk about exactly what turns him on. That doesn't mean asking, "Did you enjoy that?" after a sexual encounter. It's far too easy to avoid answering honestly for fear of hurting feelings. You must open yourself and be prepared to hear things you might not expect in order to draw out a person's true feelings about sex.

You can use a number of indirect methods to open up the discussion—such as books, movies, games, etc. Use any opportunity to tell your lover what it is you really like, whether it's in a fantasy or a real encounter. Hints and innuendo don't work when it comes to sex. And don't tease him about sexual things he does or doesn't do. Teasing isn't talking, it's a subtle form of condescension and that's the quickest way to inhibit anyone.

Both of you need to keep open minds and refrain from getting sidetracked into other areas of your relationship while discussing sex. And don't fall into the trap of talking about sex only when you have a problem. Discussion should be used to enhance your sexual experience with your lover; and if it's always negative, eventually neither one of you will want to talk about sex, much less have it.

Talking During Sex
A little talking goes a long, long way with most people. But that's a completely individual response.

Find out what your lover enjoys most, and occasionally throw a spin on it. Don't always say the same things or always feel you have to say something during sex. Try a totally silent session of lovemaking. Other times, feel free to tell him everything that feels good. As with anything else, vary your pattern and you can't go wrong.

Inhibitions
Ideally, sex should be a welcome and fulfilling part of your life. A person who considers sex a natural thing is able to communicate about it more easily and enjoy a broader range of experience in sexual encounters.

If you or your lover has inhibitions about certain sex acts, or are uncomfortable with sexuality, then in order to have a fulfilling sexual experience you must discuss these delicate issues with one another. In this case more than any other, the act of allowing someone to share your intimate secrets can do more to free your sexuality than anything else.

You and your lover needn't engage in acts that are incompatible with your values, but you owe it to each other to explore the way each of you feels. You also owe it to each other not to judge preferences as immoral or perverted. Just as you could never completely understand sexual intercourse when you were a virgin, you won't be able to understand, and therefore judge, any variation you haven't tried or fantasized about. If you can keep an open mind, and are able to trust your partner, there's a good chance you'll be surprised by your own reaction.

Giving and Receiving

Obviously, sex is a combination of both giving and receiving.

A woman who only thinks about her lover's pleasure will be just as bad a lover as one who always wants to "receive." Always focusing outward teaches you to ignore your own wants and needs.

There are several different reasons why a woman may always want to "give." It can create a sense of control. Some women have the mistaken notion that the way to get his love is by catering to his every desire. Not only will you ultimately be dissatisfied, but by focusing entirely on your lover, you're depriving him of an essential part of his sexual experience—giving to you.

Giving and receiving can actually be a good way to vary your sexual encounters. Have entire encounters with one partner completely giving and the other receiving. The next time, switch it around. You don't need to keep a mental tally sheet of who's done what to whom, trading fellatio for cunnilingus, for example. And don't feel like you have to even up the score every time he gives you a massage. Sex is a mutual act, and the giving and receiving should flow together in a continuous, harmonious cycle.

Teaching Your Lover

To have a fulfilling sexual relationship, you have to incorporate both your experience as well as your lover's. If your lover has had more experience, then consider yourself lucky. This is a chance to expand your sexual horizons. And even if your lover is less experienced than you, he will have his own contributions—just as you have something special to give a more experienced partner.

If your lover is hesitant about doing something sexual, he probably doesn't have an actual aversion to it. It's more likely he's never done it before and he doesn't want to be awkward or bad at it. Or admit he hasn't done it.

You have a wonderful opportunity when this occurs. You can broaden your lover's sexual experience. First, explain what it is that you would like to do, how you would do it, and what it feels like. Mystery and sex are a psychologically compelling couple, but when you are introducing your lover to something he isn't familiar with, you owe it to both of you to be as explicit as possible. After that, don't pressure your lover. Give him time to adjust to the new ideas. After all, you want him to want this. You know you wouldn't want pressure to do something new.

Your primary responsibility in a sexual encounter is to be open. It is a mutual experience, and it will only be complete if there is an exchange made between both of you.

Fantasies

Fantasy has a large part to play in everyone's sex life. Fantasies are used to control or stimulate sexual responses, and often a person's fantasies are the truest indicator of their desires. If you encourage your lover to reveal his innermost fantasies, you will receive a much deeper understanding of his sexual responses.

The easiest way to get your lover to discuss his fantasies is by telling him some of yours. With such an intimate topic, both of you will feel better if there is a balance struck in the information that is revealed.

Most people will start out with a very simple, "acceptable" fantasy. Fear of rejection or judgment is very real when fantasies are revealed. Often this is because fantasies deal with taboos or situations that a person wouldn't want to be involved with in real life.

But that's what fantasies are—an outlet for impulses that are not acceptable to society. You don't ever have to govern or censor your own fantasies. There is nothing to be ashamed of in yourself. It's part of you and part of the twisting and shaping that takes place in the development of your personality. Understanding and accepting yourself is the key to sexual fulfillment.

You may not be completely aware of your own fantasies—they can unwind in your mind on nearly a subliminal level, with certain undefined cues triggering your sexual response. If you can articulate these to your lover, you'll gain a much greater understanding of yourself at the same time. Are there patterns or certain scenes that strike a cord? Do you enjoy scenes of domination, humiliation, submission, breaking taboos?...Only by being completely honest and willing to explore your most basic reactions will you uncover the things that motivate you, not only sexually but in the rest of your life as well.

Aside from knowledge gained, sharing your fantasies will deepen the intimacy between you and your lover. The trust involved in sharing fantasies will help form a basis for a real and loving relationship.

Role Playing
Good communication is necessary before you can act out a fantasy. It is essential to delineate the parameters and define your roles before you begin. It can be as minor as designating one of you to be the aggressor in seducing the other. Or you can pick different personalities, character types from books or history, or stereotypes, and see what

happens when you come together. Or you can turn your fantasy into a full-fledged production, complete with costumes and dialogue.

Many people find that they experience a sense of release by acting out their fantasies. It's a better way to introduce a wider range of sex acts in your encounters than by simply suggesting one out of the blue. If you've always wanted to tie up your lover, a nonthreatening way to suggest it is by telling him about your bondage fantasy. If he is receptive and excited by your fantasy, then you can suggest that you enact it together.

Keep in mind that not all fantasies are meant to be acted out. If your lover is uncomfortable with the idea, then it's best to keep the topic on a discussion level rather than trying to hurry the process. You can explain in greater detail what it is that excites you about a certain fantasy. If you are nonjudgmental and understanding of each other, then acting out your fantasies will be an exciting, intriguing experience.

Primary Fantasy

Often people develop a certain fantasy wherein satisfaction is obtained through a series of specific actions and thoughts. The "Saturday Evening–Missionary Position" type of sex can be considered a sexual ritual, in that the same behavior is performed to the exclusion of other forms of sexual expression. Other people make fetishes or an alternative form of sexual encounter the focus of their sexual satisfaction.

When one fantasy becomes of primary importance, it can be so structured that it is impossible to fulfill every detail. If you do have a primary sexual fantasy in your life, you owe it to your lover and yourself to be open to enjoying the variations in a number of sexual activities.

Foreplay

Foreplay, of course, begins with words and gestures of attraction. Don't under estimate the power of conversation for inflaming desire in someone. Even if your lover doesn't seem interested in talking about sexual preferences or fantasies, do it anyway. Not only is it necessary to find out if you are compatible, but it's pure titillation to talk about sex before you have it.

When it comes to the physical side of foreplay, most women hate it when a man simply aims for their breasts and maybe gives their clitoris a rub or two, then expects them to be ready for sex. But that's how many women approach men. Instead of touching and exploring every part of their lover's body, they zero right in on the penis and ignore everything else.

Sure, the penis is packed with nerves and it feels great when it's touched, but it severely limits your sexual encounters when you focus exclusively on his genitals. Also, it can give the impression that you're trying to rush the sexual encounter along.

When you start touching your lover, avoid his penis at first. Even if he has an erection, it can be very exciting when a woman caresses every other part of her lover's body with her tongue and hands before she finally brushes her lips or the tips of her fingers against his penis. A long slow tease will inflame anyone.

Massage
Massage is a way to touch, savor and understand your lover's body. There are many different techniques of message, from those found in the *Kama Sutra* to modern *shiatsu*. But sexual massage is a free-form art, which should be adapted to each situation and person. Whether it's an upright rub, with your lover witting or standing, or a full-

out affair with him naked and stretched out on your bed, massage is a nonthreatening, sexual way to touch.

There are three basic methods of massage:

Stroking, with the palm or fingers of your hand. This can be done lightly or firmly, in short or long strokes. Stroking relaxes muscles and improves circulation to the small surface blood vessels. It is also thought to increase the flow of blood towards the heart.

Pressing, which includes kneading and squeezing. Pressing is usually targeted at particular muscles and joints. Remember to keep your fingers together and stiffened and slanted when pressing. You can use the tips, the heel of your hand, or the pad of your thumb.

Percussion, in which the sides of the hands are used to strike the skin. This can be done rapidly or slowly, in varying degrees of strength. Percussion improves circulation.

Massage can be anything from a quick rub at your coffee machine, to a sensual encounter complete with soft lights, music, and oil. The casual rub can be done fully dressed, while a full body massage manipulates every part of the naked body. There are also hand and foot massages, and scalp massages. Any type of massage can be given without sexual overtones or can be fully satisfying foreplay.

Like anything else, massage is a learned skill. You have to do it to get better at it. And while you are doing it, listen to the feedback your lover gives you.

Petting
Good petting isn't just aimed at the genitals. You've got two whole bodies to play with—explore every part of them.

Full body contact is important, too, either lying down or standing up. Some people simply call this cuddling. It's an easy way to get used to how your bodies feel together. You and your lover may actually be more comfortable with your clothes on—and there's a certain titillation in touching your lover sexually while you're both still dressed.

Also, there's nothing to keep you from rubbing and touching each other until you climax. Petting is a viable alternative to intercourse—and neither of you has to worry about disease or contraception. Even if you do engage in sexual intercourse, occasionally change your routine by petting to climax. For your lover, the tension of not being able to insert his penis will drive him crazy with desire. It will do you both good.

Masturbation

Masturbation is a healthy part of your sexual life. There are two good reasons to masturbate—to give yourself erotic pleasure and to help you discover more about your own sexual responses.

Men and women all masturbate to some degree or another. Most people are just reserved about admitting it. Masturbation is often considered to be something meant to be kept hidden and private. But if you're engaged in sexual intercourse, the most intimate act two people can do together, you can certainly share a little self-stimulation.

Masturbating with or in front of your lover can greatly enhance your intimacy by opening an enormous, untapped range of sexual interaction. Either as an alternative to intercourse or as part of an encounter, masturbation can be as fully shared and explored with your lover as different positions or sexual acts. Your lover will learn about your sexual responses by watching you masturbate, and you'll be better able to understand the way he likes his penis touched and the degree of pressure, strokes, and rhythms he prefers.

Intercourse should not be the primary goal of every sexual encounter. If you always end up with intercourse, there will be no suspense in your sexual relationship.

Oral Sex

Your mouth is an extremely sensitive organ. With it you are able to taste, touch, and smell your lover's body. In fact, your mouth is a lot like your genitals—rich in nerve endings and very receptive to stimulation. It makes sense for two people to bring their mouths and their genitals together.

Some people are put off by the closeness between the sex organs and the organs of excretion. The penis is used for urinating as well as sex, and there may be some concern that it is contaminated by urine. Men usually have the general idea that there's someplace in a woman's crotch that urine comes from, perhaps even contaminating the whole area.

However, urine is a sterile fluid. Sexual secretions such as sperm and the lubricating fluids from the vagina are harmless protein substances. With ordinary hygiene, the sex organs can be as germ-free and clean as any other part of the body. In fact, the mouth usually contains a great many more germs than the penis or the vulva.

If you or your lover are still worried about cleanliness, then take a shower together! It's wonderful foreplay to scrub down every inch of your lover, then have him tenderly wash every part of you. There will be no question in your mind that both of you are squeaky clean.

After cleanliness, it's usually just a lack of knowledge about each other's genitals that keeps people from enjoying oral sex. Learn by looking, touching, and talking about what feels good.

Cunnilingus

Don't be worried or feel embarrassed if your lover seems hesitant to perform cunnilingus. You may simply have to show him that your genitals are an accepted and familiar part of your body. If you don't like touching your genitals in front of him, you're not in the right frame of mind to enjoy him touching you, much less kissing you there.

A man who doesn't initiate cunnilingus usually just hasn't learned enough about a woman's sexual organs. This is definitely not an area you want to be mysterious in. Touch yourself and expose yourself for him. Masturbate for him or just spread your legs and stroke yourself. Show him how you like to be stimulated and enjoy yourself at the same time. Most people love to watch, and you'll never go wrong by showing off in front of your lover. He'll want to be right in there touching and stroking, too.

Accept your own body and revel in it, and he will. Unless they've been shown by a woman, most men won't know much about a woman's crotch. They don't know how sensitive the clitoris can be, or that the outer lips can be tugged or stroked more roughly than the inner lips.

Don't hesitate to give gentle advice and suggestions. Don't let him keep on doing something that isn't comfortable. You'll never have a better chance to adjust his technique gracefully than during the first few times he gives you cunnilingus.

Also, get to know your own scent and how it changes with the variations in your discharge. The lubricating fluids in the vagina have a distinctive smell and taste that varies in each woman. Since it is so closely associated with intercourse, many men are turned on by this scent. Other men aren't. Accept it as a natural part of being a woman, and ten-to-one your lover will share your attitude.

Fellatio

Watching a man masturbate himself is the best way to find out how he likes to have his penis touched. And talk to him about his genitals. Even if you have lots of experience with fellatio, each man is different. Like your own genitals, a man's penis and scrotum are more sensitive in some areas than in others. Only he can tell you. So watch and listen, and learn what suits your lover.

Oral sex is simply a part of your exploration of his body

using your tongue, lips, and hands. Most men like being stroked, licked, and surrounded by your mouth, as well as feeling light pressure from sucking. Use your palms and fingers on his penis, but also touch his stomach and run your hands along his thighs and buttocks. Don't forget the scrotum, with strokes from fingertips to fingernails. Some men also like to be touched on the bridge of flesh between the base of the scrotum and the anus. The anus itself is sensitive, with many nerve endings, and the pleasure of fellation can be increased when it is stimulated.

Give him feedback during oral sex. Tell him what he feels like and what he's doing that turns you on. You don't have to go overboard, but a little positive reinforcement will go a long way. He'll remember how good it felt and will be more likely to return the compliments when he gives you oral sex.

What about "deep throating"? Men say there is a certain psychological thrill that comes from inserting the entire penis into a lover's mouth. The lover's lips against the skin and hair at the base of the penis and the moist contact with the back of her throat are usually enough. But to the penis, the mouth is a big open cavern and doesn't provide continuous stimulation all along the shaft. So this technique is best appreciated as a sort of "climax" to fellatio.

Some women find it difficult to stifle the gag reflex that is triggered when something is pushed against the back of the throat. But if the head is tilted back, like a sword swallower's, the mouth and throat are brought in alignment and the gagging reflex will be considerably lessened.

Swallowing
There's no right answer. But ideally, everyone wants every aspect of his body to be accepted and cherished. Spitting out your lover's semen or not allowing him to come in your mouth will cause most men to experience some feeling of rejection.

Swallowing a man's semen is often considered one of the ultimate forms of acceptance. Most men love it and are more likely to reciprocate with a greater willingness to accept every aspect of your body.

But sometimes it doesn't taste good. Diet has a lot to do with it. Men who drink caffeinated beverages or alcohol tend to have semen that is more bitter. Protein or the lack of protein in a man's diet can also change the taste. But eating lots of fruit can make a man's semen sweeter.

Also, what's good enough for you is good enough for him. Some men have tried their own semen. Scoop up some on your finger and feed it to him, or give him a deep kiss after oral sex so he can taste himself on you. The idea is to break down the barriers between you, and nothing does that quicker than complete acceptance of your own bodies and their functions.

Remember, though, that the AIDS virus can be carried in semen. Unless you know your partner is not infected with HIV, don't let him ejaculate in your mouth. For complete safety, using a condom is recommended for oral sex.

69

Some people are talented enough to be able to give oral sex while receiving it. Others think it's crazy to ruin such a wonderful feeling by trying to concentrate on something else at the same time. It's purely a personal decision, so ask and explore. There's plenty of positions you can try or you can include mutual stimulation as a brief interlude before moving onto something else.

Intercourse

Variety

The key to mutually satisfying sexual intercourse is spontaneity. You have unlimited freedom to create a sexual encounter, from a "quickie" to an evening-long seduction. Fit your sexual encounters to the ambience. If you have intercourse in the kitchen, there won't be a lot of romance going on—more like hot, raw sex under the fluorescent lights. Or you can create a sensual atmosphere for a slow, erotic session by dimming the lights, using candles, or lighting a fire.

Don't get in the habit or always doing the same thing just because it's familiar and comfortable. It will quickly become boring, and you won't even realize it until you catch yourself thinking that sex is too much trouble or not worth the effort. Falling into a rut is the beginning of the end for your sexual relationship.

Don't have sex only on the bed. It may not be as comfortable on the rug or couch, but since when did comfort become the main goal of sex? Your sofa may be the perfect height for you to sit on the very edge as your lover penetrates you. Tables and counters are great for leaning over. That nice window seat may be the perfect thing to kneel on.

You can also help control the rhythm by being on top or putting your hands on his hips, good for either slowing him down or pulling him in harder. Varying the thrusts can change the entire tone of the sexual encounter, from slow and lazy to quick and hot. Don't let him always dictate the rhythm and don't stick with one tempo all the time, just as you don't want to use the same position for intercourse every time.

Positions

The "missionary position" usually refers to both partners stretched out on a horizontal surface, man on top. The main variables come in with the positioning of the woman's legs. You can bend your knees and brace your feet against the bed. This allows you to push against his thrust. In this position, both of you will be able to move together, neither of you completely controlling the rhythm. Or you can wrap your legs around his hips and upper thighs or bring your legs all the way forward, bracing them against his shoulders. This allows deeper penetration than the normal missionary position. Your hips will also be pinned against the bed, letting him control the rhythm.

Or the woman can be on top, straddling the man's hips as he lies or sits down. This is a position that lends itself to moving together. Many men like it because it leaves their hands free for caressing. Or he can grip your waist or hips to help control the rhythm. You can also lean forward to change the angle of penetration.

Then there's rear entry, with both of you facing the same direction. Standing, kneeling, or lying down, there are more variations than you can count. Again, some men like this position simply because it leaves their hands free to caress you or hold your hips.

Anal Eroticism

Anal intercourse is something both partners have to want to do before it can be really successful. A lot of men like to perform anal intercourse because the tight muscles in the rectum give a powerful stimulation that is different from the sensation of the vagina. Unless the recipient is relaxed, it will be impossible to penetrate the muscles in the anus without causing both pain and damage. Lubricant will ease the insertion.

Any position used for vaginal intercourse can be used for anal intercourse. The same reasons apply for switching around the positions—to allow each of you a chance to control the rhythm.

Explore anal eroticism in a gradual way. Start with fingers and work your way slowly up to anal intercourse.

It's a good idea to clean yourself before anal intercourse. It wil cut down on infection if your rectum is clean of fecal material before exposed to stress on the lining. And lastly, always wear a condom. AIDS aside, the anus is not padded with the thick lining that the vagina has. Small tears occur in the lining of the anus. In addition, very virulent bacteria live in the anus. Once you engage in anal intercourse, the penis must be washed before it is inserted in the vagina or the bacteria can cause a very bad infection.

Where

Your lover can get more excitement from where and when you have sex than how you have sex. Keep it new and exciting, even if it means having intercourse in different rooms of your house or whispering how much he turns you on while you're in a crowded room.

Sex is a sensual experience, and sensuality is heightened when you are using all your senses. You limit yourself when you limit the surroundings in which you have sex. You'll never know how exciting it can be to have sex in a place that is unusual until you try it.

Any place in the world is a potential place to have sex. It might turn out to be uncomfortable or hurried, but the sheer eroticism of having intercourse in a car, or outdoors, or in the bathroom at a party, is worth every inconvenience. You wouldn't want to give up the comfort and privacy of your own bedroom, but if you seize the moment you will have an experience that will be memorable.

You can either plan your sex in unusual places, or it can be spontaneous. It's actually easier to take advantage of the chance opportunities that fall your way. It may not always be romantic, but it will be erotic.

Don't hold back for fear of being "caught." Don't hesitate to suggest it when you see a good place or time to make love. Even if you don't do it every time, the mere suggestion and the knowledge that you *might* will be titillation enough.

By consistently telling your lover how much you are

attracted to him and want to have sex with him, you will do a great deal to furthering your sexual relationship. If you reserve sex for special occasions or a certain place, you will be isolating it from the rest of your relationship.

When
As with any other aspect, don't always have sex at the same time of day or the same day every week.

Women's body chemistry fluctuates in two main cycles— the day, and the four-week menstrual cycle. Your sexual response and experience will change along with these cycles.

You owe it to yourself to pay attention to your menstrual cycle and learn how your sexual response varies with the hormonal changes. Ovulation occurs approximately fourteen days after the start of the last menstruation. Often women experience food cravings or light crampings when they ovulate. Your body is chemically altered to urge you to have sex. You can either make the most of this hormone-induced aphrodisiac, or be unaware of its subliminal promptings. Your body will also change with the onset of every menstruation, particularly in breast and uterine swelling and tenderness.

The subtle changes in the rhythms of your body throughout the day and their affects on your sexual response can also be explored. Particularly with a new lover, experience sex at different times of the day. Some people are unresponsive in the mornings or late at night when they're tired, while other times they can hardly hold back. You need to get to know your own as well as your lover's rhythms and preferences.

Sexual Aids

Sexual aids are objects that are used to enhance your sexual encounters, whether it's sexy clothing, satin sheets, erotica, toys, aphrodisiacs…Almost anything can be used to add variety to sex—and since monotony is the death of sex, explore some of these options.

Clothing

Men like women to wear nice underwear that accents their bodies. It doesn't have to be expensive or fancy, but if your bras and underpants are old or don't fit well or are ugly, it can be a real turn-off. Your lover sees your undies as part of your attitude toward yourself, and will wonder how you can feel attractive wearing something tattered and worn. Besides, you take time and effort to look good for the rest of the world, don't you want to give your lover an even better surprise?

Sexy clothing is also an excellent way to vary your sexual encounters. As your relationship progresses, the two of you can choose sexy clothing together. This can be an erotic experience in itself. Mail order catalogs for both men and women are especially good for this; you can follow through on the titillation right then and there.

Pay attention to what your lover says about you and accent the features he admires. But don't let that stop you from walking around in high heels and a T-shirt even if it's breasts he likes. Give him a chance to appreciate every part of you.

Aphrodisiacs

Hundreds of drinks and foods have been credited with erotic power at one time or another. Oysters, quail eggs, ginger, chocolate, and more. However, most of these items are useful because of their association with sex, rather than the physical property of arousing sexuality.

Even Spanish fly, or cantharides, the most famous aphrodisiac, doesn't create a sexual reaction in your body. In fact, many of the powders and mixtures sold as aphrodisiacs aren't healthy and can be downright dangerous. Don't even try these things.

Alcohol can remove your inhibitions, but too much can have the reverse effect. The user can become moody and depressed, and physical sensations are blunted, making erections chancy.

Marijuana is a mild depressant, relaxing both the mind and body, releasing inhibitions and inducing a mild euphoria. If you are feeling sexy, it can make intercourse a highly erotic experience because visual and tactile perceptions are often enhanced. But for some people, marijuana is far too relaxing to make for good sex. In some states, even a small amount of marijuana is illegal.

Amyl nitrate, also called "poppers," are little capsules that you break and inhale. Butyl nitrite products are sold as liquid incense or room odorizers, but they produce the same effect as the prescription amyl nitrate. Poppers relax blood vessels, decreasing blood pressure and giving the user a warm, floating sensation. Both amyl nitrite and butyl break down the immune system with prolonged exposure.

The drug called "Ecstacy" is reputed to enhance the sexual experience. However, its long term health effects are unknown, and this designer drug isn't recommended.

Cocaine, like every other drug, can have vastly different effects on people, depending on body chemistry. Some men swear by cocaine, saying it prolongs and enhances the sexual experience. But for other men, cocaine tends to wreck havoc with an erection. Cocaine is also an illegal drug.

Sex Toys

Like any other gimmick, you can rapidly tire of using sex toys. But even if they give you a couple of nights of amusement and sexy fun, they're worth it.

Vibrators and dildos. These are probably the most common sex toys. Vibrators are great, for both men and women. You hold the vibrator against your genitals or you can insert it into the vagina—or rub it anywhere on your body to feel its tingling, relaxing vibration. They come in various shapes and sizes and run on batteries to create the vibration.

The intensity of a vibrator makes it a wonderful masturbation tool, and it's an excellent way for women who have difficulty with climaxing to learn how. Contrary to popular belief, a woman can't become addicted to her vibrator—the more you learn about your own responses and how it feels, the easier it will be to achieve orgasm.

Dildos are stiff, phallic-shaped objects that are used for vaginal or anal stimulation. The size depends on which area it is to be used for.

If you use a homemade dildo, make certain it is clean, whether it's a cucumber or a carrot. Always have a cap on empty bottles. The in-and-out movement can cause strong suction to develop, and you may find that you can't remove the bottle without causing damage to a woman's uterus.

Ben-wa Balls. Ben-wa balls, or Japanese love balls, are another sex toy. They are two weighted balls that a woman inserts into her vagina. The sensation the movement of the balls create are supposed to excite the woman as she moves. Most women find the effect to be less than they had hoped for.

Cock Rings. A cock ring is a circle of flexible material that is placed at the base of the penis. As the penis becomes erect, the cock ring traps the blood, so that hardness is prolonged. For some men, a cock ring can add intense pleasure to an orgasm; others find it painful

Erotica. Erotica includes sexually oriented books, pictures, and movies. Many people enjoy using any or all of these forms of erotica as an occasional stimulant prior to or during sex.

Movies. With the advent of the VCR, it is very common

and convenient to rent X-rated movies and view them at home. X-rated movies can be taken in a humorous light, yet the sight of other people engaging in sex—no matter how artificially enacted—can be stimulating.

Magazines. Erotic magazines feature stills of nude men or women. Some that come in plastic wrap and cost more show various forms of intercourse, come shots, mixed-race-and-gender-sex—you name it, they have a magazine for it. Aren't you curious? Like videos, these can be both humorous and stimulating. They are especially useful for masturbation.

Some women feel insecure about a lover's looking at these sorts of magazines. But don't turn away from this rich source of pleasure. Share the experience with your lover. Flip through the magazine and point out the pictures you like. Tell him why—you've always wanted to try sex in this position or you wish you looked like that. Use it as a way to open up communication between both of you.

Books. Erotic books range from material written hundreds of years ago to the flimsy bodice rippers of today. Books are less shared activity than pictures, but reading such literature can only expand your knowledge and acceptance of the astounding variety of human sexual experience. Buy erotic books for yourself as well as your lover. Anais Nin erotica as well as her diaries are an excellent choice for beginners. Nin saw sex from a sensualist's viewpoint and reflects the woman's sensibility in her writing.

Using Your VCR Camera

Home movies were never like this! Buy or rent a video camera and let the fun begin.

It can add a real spark to know that your every move is being captured. You'll be surprised at the result. You don't have to be a great actor—your real reactions and feelings will come through better than any performance you might put on.

Filming yourselves is just half of the fun. Watch the film with your lover as foreplay for your next sexual encounter. It's better than a porno flick anytime.

4 | *Playing With Power*

The Meaning of Playing With Power

Everyone's personality has both dominant and submissive tendencies. The way in which these elements are expressed varies from person to person, depending on a given situation and background.

Human beings have evolved very rapidly, but we still have many of the primitive instincts and traits we once needed to survive in a more dangerous world. Society, for the protection of the whole, attempts to channel these aggressive tendencies into a wide range of activities, including spectator sports, exercise programs, hobbies, etc. Yet human biological impulses can't be denied. The desire to control our environment is conditioned into acceptable behavior, but without adequate release, this strong desire often becomes linked with another basic drive—sexuality.

Giving up control or taking complete control of your partner in a sexual encounter can be the ultimate catharsis. A person's entire personality can be distorted by suppressed desires trying to work their way past walls and blocks that were erected in childhood. Accepting and exploring these impulses with a trusted lover can be the healthiest way to release conflicted tensions.

To grant power or receive it, there must be consent between the participants. To take power is not an exchange—it's rape or abuse. But if both of you discuss the exchange and establish parameters, then you can play with power in a very real, psychological, and satisfying way. The power exchange is not a lifelong commitment. It lasts for as long as the sexual encounter lasts; then the two participants return to a state of equilibrium.

Dominant/Submissive

The partner in control of the scene is usually referred to as the dominant, while the partner who relinquishes control is considered the submissive. In alternative forms of sexual interaction, such as SM, often the terms "top" and "bottom" are used.

There is a definite dominant-submissive quality to any sort of sexual interaction. Playing with power exchange is simply a way of openly acknowledging that fact between two lovers. Once you accept that, then you and your partner are free to try almost anything within the boundaries you have established for your power play.

Society's Roles

The patriarchal structure currently in place has been challenged, but its dictates are still seen in the feminine ideal of passivity, in traditional love stories, and in the limitations of the corporate workplace. Women are conditioned to be submissive to those in power, and have long achieved their own desires with techniques that are less than overt. Men still hold most positions of primary importance, a condition that carries intense expectations and pressures that many men suffer under.

Women. Whether it's through sexual power play or by simply getting their lover to do what they want, many women regard the dominant role as their just returns. Often it's seen as an expression of power that is denied by mainstream society. When you dominate a man, it's a strong affirmation that you can control the events in your life to get what you need. It's an expression of freedom—a defiant and self-fulfilling gesture of independence.

Then again, society's conditioning does play a major role in the development of a woman's personality. Women are taught to equate love and romance with surrendering control and subordinating themselves to a man. Many women are taught to expect that a knight on a white horse will appear and sweep them off their feet, taking them off to high adventure and the tenderest of romances while protecting them completely. Even if you recognize and reject this ideal as impractical and impossible, it still permeates every relationship. You may know that your lover has all the faults and insecurities of any average person and that he isn't a "knight"...but you still may find yourself thinking that if he just did *this* or *that* he'd be so much closer to what you always dreamed of having.

So women are conditioned with this desire, yet are given no practical way to satisfy it. By playing with power exchange, you can give up your control to a trusted lover and fulfill this desire within the parameters of a sexual encounter. You can use power exchange to recognize tendencies in your personality that are born of this conditioning— reactions and mannerisms you've acquired to relinquish power and subordinate yourself to another. Creating a sexual encounter where this can be done requires a constructive, controlled environment. Within the encounter, you can channel your submissive desires, soothing subconscious proddings that can otherwise interfere with your ability to overtly take control in every other aspect of your life.

Men. Men are expected to be dominant, powerful, successful, sensitive, protective, caring, etc.... Who can live up to such an image? For many men, the submissive role gives them the chance to relinquish the responsibility and stress of always having to make sense of a complex world. It's very comforting and relaxing when someone else takes complete control for a while. Most men don't get the chance to do this in a loving environment; instead they are chafing under the restrictions of family members or a dominating boss in the workplace.

Some men enjoy being submissive to women because they truly believe that women are more powerful than men. Perhaps this rests on the "mother image"—that the most powerful being in their world as they developed personalities and consciousness was a woman. Some men re-experience that sense of safety and comfort they had as protected infants by giving up control to a trusted partner.

On the other hand, men can also enjoy being completely in control in the same way women enjoy relinquishing control—it's what society has trained us to want. No woman will ever give up complete control to a man, yet he has learned to desire that and feel complete as a man when he has it. His ego yearns for it, and it can be satisfied through an exchange of power in a sexual encounter.

Submissives

It's important to understand why an individual wishes to take the role of submissive. A dominant who understands the psychological workings of the submissive will be better able to satisfy these needs.

The submissive can be a person who is normally aggressive in the rest of life and is looking for a release of the suppressed side of the personality. For these people, taking a submissive role in a sexual exchange is a positive way to explore all aspects of their personality.

Other submissives are those who are always found in the role of giving, caring, making do, etc. For these people, expressing their submissive tendencies in the sexual arena can allow them to take a more aggressive role in their careers or relationships. Role-playing may help them recognize certain types of behavior that are hindering them in real life.

For some, playing a submissive role fulfills a need for

acceptance. Within a scene, the submissive is "owned" by the dominant, thereby confirming the inherent worth of the submissive. After all, people protect and treasure the objects they own.

There also can be an exhibitionist quality about submissives. They are being watched, touched, manipulated, and caressed by the dominant. Being submissive can be the ultimate in narcissistic pleasure.

Another element of the submissive experience is the desire to push the limits of experience, to be able to take whatever one is ordered to take. Endurance is proof of the submissive's strength of will.

Dominants

There is a seductive power in controlling another human being, even if it is only for a limited time. Dominants can take pleasure and pride in watching the submissive's reaction, knowing that they are the cause.

Some dominants enjoy the possession of their submissive's, treating them like a treasure to be thoroughly enjoyed. The dominant also has free rein to touch or manipulate the submissive's body in any way they desire.

Many dominants are naturally aggressive people. They may exert great control in all areas of their lives, or they may wish to, while being thwarted in one way or another. These people will enjoy being able to dominate in the sexual arena.

Other dominants are unsure of themselves and are searching for confirmation that they do have control—even if it is only in a sexual encounter. This type of dominant doesn't usually enjoy the idea of playing the role of submissive because it seems to confirm personal insecurities.

Safe-word

When you are engaged in dominant-submissive activity, it is essential to the spirit of consensuality that the submissive has a signal that will end the scene. If fantasy or role-playing is involved, the submissive will often want to say, "no" or "stop," and struggle as hard as possible without really wanting the scene to end. Yet if there is true discomfort—from pain or mental abuse that is not desired—the submissive must have a safe-word that is used only as a way to stop the scene.

For everyone, there are certain types of submission that are not pleasant or titillating or that are genuinely uncomfortable. If the submissive doesn't want an activity, then to inflict it is a form of nonconsensual abuse, like wife beating or child abuse. Hence, the safe-word is the key to keeping your dominant-submissive interaction firmly in the arena of consensuality.

The use of the safe-word is not a capitulation to the dominant, such as "mercy" or "uncle." One of the primary enjoyments derived from dominant-submissive activities is the drawing out of a voluntary submission, with the submissive receiving great pleasure from capitulation. This doesn't necessarily mean the end of the scene, but the use of the safe-word does.

Some dominants argue that this puts ultimate control of the scene in the submissive's hands. That's true regardless of a safe-word. Those who have had a negative experience at the hands of another should never allow themselves to be put in a helpless position again. That is the ultimate control—submissives *allow* others to dominate them. Responsible dominants only do so with a partner's consent. A safe-word ensures that both participants remain equals, despite any activity that's taken place.

A last suggestion—choose a safe-word that sounds unique so that it can't be confused with something else. And pick one you like so you can stick with it. That way, you and your partner won't forget what it is.

Setting Up a Scene

Setting the scene is very simple, really. It's a game. And like any game, discussing the rules is the way to layout the framework of the activity. A safe-word is necessary, as well as an understanding of what type of interaction the submissive is looking for, and what in particular is *not* wanted. Discussing your favorite fantasies is the best way to get an idea of your true desires.

The atmostphere is best if it is comfortable and relaxed. That usually depends on the amount of trust between the participants. The more trust, the more pure the thrill will be for all involved.

So, set up a safe-word and do your best to eliminate distractions. After that, it's up to the imagination of the dominant.

How to Dominate

The most important thing to remember about dominating someone is that you are in control. Your insecurities, your problems, your worries can be completely put aside. For this span of time, the scene will unfold solely according to your desire. You have the freedom to do anything until the scene ends—either at your discretion or at the submissive's safe-word.

This knowledge of complete control will give you the confidence and attitude that will stimulate any submissive. If the scene is the enactment of a particular fantasy, then talk the role, act the role, be what it is you want to be. If the scene is simply one of stimulation and control, then do things that excite you. Do things that produce a reaction that you enjoy. The scene is yours, and your submissive will appreciate that psychological factor more than any action you might perform.

Play With the Senses

The erotic experience is a sensual one, so play with all the senses: taste, touch, smell, hearing, and sight. Combining and creating different sensations of different intensities will keep interaction from becoming predictable or routine.

Submissives can be blindfolded; or made to sit or stand in a certain way or place. Their mouths can be gagged. Hands tied. Bodies manipulated, stimulated with pleasure or tickling or pain. The possibilities are endless—which makes this a powerful, enduring source of pleasure.

As with any alternative form of sexual interaction, these suggestions are most enjoyed when the subject has been discussed between the partners, even the most abstract way. Fantasies, day dreams, scenes from movies and books can be used to determine what elements are most titillating to you and your partner.

Bondage

Scarves, ties, belts, rope, leather cuffs...bondage is a wonderful expression of dominance-submission. It is a symbolic act of complete submission for one person to allow another to restrain him or her.

The most tricky aspect of a bondage scene is the element of fear. If the submissive partner doesn't enjoy the idea of intimidation, enjoyment may be totally destroyed by feeling truly threatened. Other submissives receive intense pleasure from a sense of apprehension; the greater the fear the better.

Some people like the aesthetics of bondage, the way the ropes or cloth or leather crosses the skin, exposing certain parts and concealing others. Others like the immobility that bondage brings. Whatever the preference—there are hundreds of ways to bind your lover.

Exhibitionism/Voyeurism

Watching or being watched: Everyone gets a certain amount of pleasure from both aspects. Being admired is a wonderful sensation, and so is simply watching your lover run around the house while scantily dressed or nude.

Men are trained to be visually oriented, but here's where you can use it to your advantage. Cultivate your exhibitionist tendencies. Don't hide your body—revel in it, share it with him, let him admire you. Sure, what woman doesn't want to lose or gain a few pounds? Complaining about your flaws and hiding your body because it isn't perfect eliminates a vital part of a man's sexual pleasure.

Nurture your lover's exhibitionist tendencies as well. As you share your own body, partake of his. If you're dominating a man with a desire to exhibit himself, then tell him to reveal his body to you. Every part of it.

Shaving
The act of shaving hair off the body can be very sensual. There's the water and slippery soap or shaving cream. Then there's the feel of the razor as it slips effortlessly over the skin. And once you're done, the part that was shaved looks completely different.

People are accustomed to seeing hair in certain places, and shaving can provide an erotic shock to the eyes. To some people, shaved skin is reminiscent of innocence and youth, stimulating feelings of protection for the dominant and vulnerability in the submissive.

Shaving is also something that stays with you for a while. The irritation as the stubble grows in depends on the tenderness of the site that was shaved. But as a dominant, you may like your submissive to have a temporary reminder of your scene.

Cross Dressing
Most women are intrigued by the feminine side of men and have tried at one time or another to put makeup on their boyfriends or held a dress up to their lover to see the effect.

Some men have difficulty expressing this desire because

it hits so squarely on conditioned taboos that men and women are different and should dress differently. But that's all it is—societal conditioning. For some men, wearing women's clothing becomes a symbolic gesture of acceptance of feelings and emotions that are traditionally reserved for women alone. It is also a form of respect—the most sincere form of flattery, after all, is imitation.

Urination
Some people get a thrill from watching their lover or being watched by their lover as they urinate. Many women are simply curious about how men urinate, just as they are curious in general about the workings of a man's penis.

Urination for women is typically very private, and to allow your lover to watch can be an intense form of intimacy.

Fetishes
A fetish is a symbol of sexuality. It can be parts of the body—breasts, penis, or foot. Or it can be clothing, such as a shoe or glove. For some people, the symbol becomes highly charged with meaning. Often fantasies are centered around these symbols, and their presence in a sexual encounter can greatly enhance the pleasure.

SM

The bias against SM is quite virulent in mainstream society, primarily because of lack of information. Yet there is a growing trend—from pop star endorsements to national magazine coverage—to open up this area of sexual interaction for general discussion and exploration.

It's said that only dysfunctional people partake in SM. People also say we don't need more abuse and hostility in the world. But SM is about sensitivity, sensuality, exploration, and understanding one's own motivations and desires. How can that be negative?

Like any other sexual encounter, SM is a sensual experience. Usually it's just more intense than traditional sex. This could be due to the intensity of sensations administered to all parts of the body, or it could be due to the direct stimulation of emotions through fantasies or role-playing. In addition, an SM relationship must contain a greater element of trust than any other form of relationship

SM Defined

First, let's define the term "SM"—or "S&M" as it's also called. The letters "SM" stand for sadism and masochism. A person is a sadist who enjoys inflicting mental or physical pain upon another. Often a sadist experiences this as a form of sexual release or gratification. Masochism is the reverse—the tendency to gain sexual gratification through the acceptance of physical abuse or humiliation. But among those who practice SM, this term has come to mean a variety of things.

Simply put, the precise definition of SM doesn't encompass the reality of the experience. SM can certainly include the giving and receiving of pain, either physical or mental, but often a scene includes one or more of the following:

1. Dominant-submissive interaction
2. Fantasy and role-playing activities
3. Fetish involvement

It is interesting to note that for many participants of SM, sex is not a necessary part of a scene. Yet, though neither partner may climax, intense satisfaction is received by both through the gratification of more primal, suppressed drives. This places SM in the "safe sex" category in this age of AIDS. However, masturbation, oral sex, or intercourse can be, and often is, included as part of an SM scene—or may immediately follow—resulting in orgasm for one or both of the partners.

It is also interesting to note that many people involved in SM do not drink alcohol or use drugs during their scenes. There's no need to relieve tension or blur reality because they have chosen to step out of reality simply by playing a role.

SM may not be the normal avenue of sexual expression in our society, but that doesn't mean it's to be shunned. Some people are simply not interested or intrigued by the idea of SM. But for those who are titillated by SM fantasies or have harbored a secret curiosity, SM could be an exciting option to add to your sexual exploration.

Pain

Some people find that pain can enhance sexual pleasure. Whether it's fingernails dragged across the skin and love bites, or deliberate, inflicted pain, if it provides pleasure for both partners, there is no reason not to indulge yourself.

Masochists are not all necessarily abused as children. Quite the contrary—many were never even spanked; yet they heard about the physical punishments their friends received and associated that intensity of parental focus to security and guidance from an all-powerful figure.

Sadists, on the other hand, often experience the power of inflicting pain as the ultimate domination of a human being.

However, people more often get sexual gratification from fantasizing about pain than actually inflicting or receiving it. The reason for this, or course, is the basic human instinct that tells us pain is to be avoided.

Yet when pain is inflicted, natural chemicals called endorphins are released from the brain. These chemical compounds are produced by the pituitary gland and elsewhere in the body. Endorphins are thought to have an effect similar to morphine, masking pain and producing euphoria.

The key to reaching this state of euphoria is to relax under the pain. Controlled, rhythmic breathing combined with an even, repetitious application of pain that steadily rises in intensity will trigger this exhilarating state.

Flagellation

Floggers, whips, belts, straps, crops, canes...

The idea is to start slowly and sensuously, and build up from there. The entire body can be stimulated by striking the skin, but avoid the area in the small of the back where the kidneys lie, as well as the tender joint areas. Also, don't allow the instrument to "wrap around" the sides of the submissive's torso, arms, and legs. This can cause a much sharper pain and leave a mark on the flesh.

Many whips are made of soft, pliable strips of leather and their affect when administered gently is not pain but caressing pleasure.

Spanking

In spanking, the pain inflicted is often not as important as the sense of humiliation and power evoked when one partner submits to the other. Then again, if you use a gloved hand or paddle, the intensity and number of smacks can increase the pain as the skin reddens and bruises.

Habitual spankers sometimes work out a ritual of misbehavior in the submissive that gives them an excuse for exercising the punishment.

Hot Wax

The sensation of hot candle wax falling on bare skin is a brief, warm pain. On contact, the wax immediately starts to cool and harden. You can alter the heat by raising or lowering the candle as you drip it. Scraping off the dried wax can be an erotic experience as well.

Beeswax candles will cause a burn because it retains its heat longer, but regular, dime store candles don't contain real beeswax and won't burn the skin.

SM Fantasies

SM is most often enjoyed by people as a form or sexual fantasy. Many people who don't wish to actually take a role as a submissive can derive intense sexual gratification from fantasizing about such a role. For some, shyness or guilt will keep them from enacting their SM tendencies, and fantasies are the only outlet they allow themselves. For others who do enjoy SM activities in their sexual encounters, SM fantasies can go much further than what they enact.

Indeed, SM fantasies often range deeply into the "unsafe" category, rendering them impossible to enact. Safe, sane, and consensual are the guidelines for any SM activity. If your fantasy involves practices that could permanently harm someone, then the fantasy is not one that can be enacted. If your fantasy includes anything nonconsensual, such as reape or molestation, then it can only be enacted if it is discussed and your partner is willing to role-play the activity with you.

Introducing the Subject to Your Lover

It can be very enlightening to note the initial response of your lover when you mention SM. People will usually say one of two things: "I don't think I could let anyone do that to me," or "I couldn't ever do that to my lover." Usually people protest against the role they would secretly prefer.

Which one was your response when you first started this section?

Finding an SM partner

Women who want to experiment with dominance can do so relatively safely. It isn't difficult to shift a sexual encounter with your lover into one that is an exchange of power which you control. Talk to your lover and find out what he fantasizes about, then simply tell him to lie back and relax.

But the woman who wants to express her submissive aspect must be careful. For the submissive woman, SM clubs and organizations are the safest way to explore SM. That way you can meet dominant men under controlled circumstances. Watch a man dominate another woman to see if you might enjoy that sort of treatment. Talk to him about what he likes about dominating women. You want a man who gives a lot of love—not someone who seeks to bolster his own ego by degrading you. Above all, SM is intended to be a sensual, pleasurable interaction that satisfies you both psychologically as well as physically.

SM Club List
The follwing list can be used to locate a club in your area.

> Backdrop. Bay area SM club with nearly 4,000 members and a large clubhouse, gift store, and magazine. Membership package $20: P.O. Box 1369, El Cerrito, CA 94530-1369 (415) 234–3617.

> Eulenspiegel Society. Well established group for SM people of all persuasions. Magazine, newsletter, and program of events: P.O. Box 2783, Grand Central Station, New York, N.Y. 10163-2783 (212) 633–TESM.

> Forum Society. National correspondence and contact society in monthly newsletter plus personal box number for advertising: SASE to P.O. Box 418, Cardiff London, CF2 4XU.

> International Ms. Leather. Nonprofit organization dedicated to linking women's leather organizations internationally: P.O. Box 460504, San Francisco, CA 94146, (415) 863–1386.

Society of Janus. Bondage, submission, domination, fetishism, SM, etc. Regular social events and magazine: P.O. Box 6794, San Francisco, CA 90291.

National Leather Association. International association of people of all sexual persuasions who are into leather and associated pleasures. A quarterly journal, local newsletters, annual conference, and a variety of social and educational activities: 584 Castro St. #44, San Francisco CA, 94114-2500, or NLA-Metro New York, P.O. Box 1084, New York, N.Y. 10156 (718) 597-0019.

Threshold. The Los Angeles SM enthusiasts' group. P.O. Box 5143, Playa Del Rey, CA 90293.

5 | *Answering Specific Questions About You and Your Man*

Questions and Answers*

A Submissive Man

Q. I had been seeing this guy for seven months when we decided to have sex. He is thirty and had lived with an older woman for four months about a year ago. I am twenty-eight and this was my first relationship. It was also the first time I had sex. The problem is that the first two times we tried he could not get an erection and I had to manually stimulate him. I didn't think anything was wrong with this because I've often heard of men sometimes not being able to get aroused. After that night he kept his distance from me. After a month he met me and told me that he thinks he's a homosexual and that that night proved it to him. He seems very confused and we are still great friends. I suggested he see someone to help him sort things out. He thinks there is no point to this even though he is still very much attracted to me and feels that he just can't say no when I'm near him. I care very much about him and would like to help him. But what can I do?

*Reprinted with permission, the *Learning Annex Magazine*, June–February 1992.

A. You were right—there is nothing wrong with manually stimulating a man to erection. Some men prefer it that way. You're also right that all that is needed in this case is sorting a few things out.

First, you say he "can't say no" when you're near him. Second, he needed you to stimulate him directly. Third, he lived with an older woman. It sounds to me like your boyfriend is sexually a submissive person. He likes it when his lover takes control. That may be why he thinks he might be a homosexual, because he's attracted to the drive and aggressiveness of men, not because he's attracted to their bodies.

You sound as if you have a caring nature— do you also have it in you to take control? Be confident that you can take this relationship where you want to go. In sexual matters, be the aggressor. Don't wait for him to make up his mind or make the first move. You said he's keeping his distance—he may simply be wanting you to take action. Just because you're inexperienced, that doesn't mean you can't use your imagination and intelligence and discover your sexuality together.

Making the First Move

Q. I met a man this past weekend at a party. We got along well but we only talked for a little while. I liked him and I think he liked me, but I think I acted distant or something because he didn't ask for my number or anything. He's a cousin to one of my friends, so I could get his number. Would I look pushy if I called him? Or should I ask my friend to give him my number?

A. Either way would do, but since it's you who are interested, it would be best if you called him. Too often, women just wait around for their dates or even their boyfriends to call them. Tell your friend you want his number, and ask her to call and let him know that she gave it to you. More than likely he'll be fine with that, then you can call him. The less your friend has to act as a go-between the better.

How to Get Affection

Q. I like to cuddle with my boyfriend, but he seems to take it for granted that I want to have sex whenever I snuggle up close. Sometimes I do and sometimes I don't. I never get more than a few seconds before he's pulling up my shirt to get to my breasts and starting to breathe hard. How do I get cuddles without giving up to sex?

A. Suggest that you both play a game. One of you will lead (start out with you), touching your lover's body while he "mirrors" your movements. This does not include intercourse; that way you can get him to do whatever you want without actually having sex. Tell him at the beginning that he's not to break out of his "mirror" or the game stops. Then really do it up right. Take your time, caressing his face and neck, running your fingers through your hair, kissing him and gazing into his eyes. If you want to, you can both lie down, and simply hold each other to your heart's content. Don't allow the cuddling to turn into sex until you're satisfied, then by all means, if you'd like that, pronounce the game ended and have fun.

Also, do yourself a favor, and later on tell your boyfriend how much you enjoyed your cuddle. Tell him you'd like to do it again sometime. If he doesn't pick up the hint, then simply play your game again. Let him lead, too. Sometimes that's the quickest way to teach someone—to allow them to take action for themselves. Either way, you're in for a lot of cuddles.

Pangs of Divorce

Q. I have a friend from work and he's been divorced for a few months. We're friends and we talk, but I want to date him and have a relationship with him. How long does it take for a man to want to start having sex after a divorce? And how do I get him to want me?

A. He likes you but he's made no move to ask you out to dinner? Have you asked him? Deepen the friendship you have established with the man. Talk to him about how he's feeling.

There's no average time limit for getting over a divorce. If your friend continues to make no move, then it's up to you to tell him that you're sexually attracted to him. You can't wait forever.

Reluctance to Orgasm

Q. My boyfriend likes to give me oral sex. When I let him, it feels good, but it usually just makes me want to have sex with him. He keeps wanting to do it until I come. He's been pushing me, and that makes me not want thim to do it at all anymove. How can I tell him that?

A. It's more important to find out why you feel the way you do rather than set limits which will keep you from discovering what might be blocking you from enjoying part of your sexual experience together. Is your boyfriend new? Maybe you aren't emotionally secure with him, or aren't sure what his feelings are toward you. You may be afraid of giving your boyfriend too much power over you by you losing control and revealing the things that you truly desire. Perhaps you doubt his reasons for wanting to give you oral sex. Or you might be more comfortable yourself with the power of giving rather than receiving.

So, ask him. Tell him to describe his perfect fantasy of giving a woman oral sex. Ask him what he's feeling as he tells you. His motivation should be fairly clear. Also, if it makes you feel better, for a while you can trade off oral sex. That way you'll feel as if you are both taking an equal share of the control.

Talking During Sex

Q. Do men like it when you talk to them during sex? It seems like it breaks the mood whenever I try it. And what about sex words and slang?

A. It can be a turn-on for your lover to hear you murmur in his ear. But don't use dirty words in such an intimate setting if he doesn't normally include them in his vocabulary. People who don't cuss are sensitive to it.

On the other hand, telling him it feels good, repeating his name, and letting out inarticulate bursts of ecstasy are completely acceptable. Maybe you're just thinking about it too much instead of letting the moment move you to speech.

Relax, and the words—as well as your groans and moans—will escape naturally. Whatever you do, try not to remain completely silent. That's cheating you both of a major sensation in the world of sex. Expressing your feelings freely can increase the excitement for you both more than any other fancy technique you may have picked up.

When Sex is Routine

Q. My girlfriend and I have been going out for eight months. At first, our lovemaking was really exciting, but it has fallen into a kind of routine. I still love her, but she's pulled back and doesn't seem as physically attracted to me anymore. Is it me? What should I do to keep her sexually interested in me?

A. Your sex life has fallen into a routine because you aren't working together to keep it exciting. And the only way you can work with someone, be it a business relationship or a sexual one, is by discussing the details.

It may seem like a difficult thing to talk about, but there is a trick to it. If you start talking about your own sexuality—your own fears, for example, that she is no longer attracted to you and what tha means to you—without being accusatory or defensive, then you will open a dialogue. Asking questions is fine, but in this case it sounds like the two of you don't have much conversation going on about your sexuality; in the beginning of such a thing it is often less threatening to give of yourself than ask for her feelings on the subject. If you begin to talk and share, I guarantee that she will soon follow your example. Then you can find out for yourself exactly what your girlfriend wants from your relationship and how both of you can get what you need.

Battered Woman

Q. My daughter, who is four years old, and I moved in with a man two years ago. His wife had left him not quite a year before and taken their two daughters with her. I love this man, and I know he has problems, but mostly what we have is special. Except sometimes when he's not happy or he says something like he's deliberatly trying to hurt me or get me away from him, then I fight with him. He says not to push him when he gets like that, but it drives me crazy. The thing is, he's started getting more violent. He's pushed me a few times, and kicked me once when I was on the ground. Then a month ago we were fighting and I knew I should have stopped, but I didn't. He threw me so hard against the wall that I got a concussion. I didn't know what to say to the hospital people. I know you aren't supposed to stay with a man who beats you, but he doesn't really. What can I do?

A. You can admit that he is violent toward you. You can accept that you have a need to discuss certain things with your lover without having him attack you. This is basic human rights here—nothing you say gives anyone the right to physically hurt you. Nothing. And if he can't restrain himself from hurting you, then you must leave him. As you said yourself—he's getting worse. The deterioration is typical of allowing yourself to be treated with such little respect. And not only that, there's your young daughter to consider. Do you really think that environment is good for her?

There is no reason to stay in a relationship once abuse has entered the picture. Get some distance between you—even if you end up working out the problems and he commits himself to treating you respectfully from now on—the only way to reach that state is to physically separate yourself from him. Nothing less will convince him you're serious about having a man who loves and esteems you or having no man at all.

Giving Constructive Criticism

Q. I showed my boyfriend an article in a magazine on improving your sex life, and he freaked out. First he asked me why I was showing it to him. Then he started talking about all the women he's satisfied and getting real defensive. I didn't like it, and he was all mad, too. How can I get him to be better in bed when he already thinks he's the best?

A. Nobody appreciates being judged, and we are often too quick to assume we are being judged when it comes to sexual matters. Just as your boyfriend reacted strongly to what he saw as criticism, you got jealous when he mentioned the other women he has pleased.

It's a fact of nature that people always hve more to learn—whether it's about sex, or relationships, or ourselves. And don't forget that we mostly learn from each other. Your boyfriend developed his sexuality in each of his relationships, just as you have in yours. Those past relationships have nothing to do with the one you're in now, except that they laid the foundation in each of you for this relationship. And that's a good thing.

If you can share the things you have learned with each other—and listen to each other's desires—then that will allow you to develop your sexuality even further together. But it is only to the extent that you draw the wealth of both past experiences into your sexual relationship that you will both be satisfied. It is a mutual experience and it will only be complete if there is an exchange made between lovers.

Helping Your Partner Cope

Q. I married a tall, slender, attractive man almost three years ago. Our relationship is good—our schedules change around so we don't spend a lot of time together like most couples do in the evenings. But we get along real well and are comfortable together. I think he's sexy, but he's put on about fifty pounds since we got married. I don't really mind, but he does. I tell him to go on a diet, or at least not eat all those sweet and fatty things he likes. He used to be much more active, so I guess that kept him thinner. I'm mostly a vegetarian, so I don't have much trouble with my weight. I don't understand how he can feel so miserable about it but not do anything. How can I help him lose weight?

A. Talk to him about it. It's common for people to overeat when they're distressed or frustrated about their lives. It could be that your husband isn't as comfortable with the split schedules as you are. Or it could be that the change in lifestyle that made him less active is depressing him emotionally as well. Only you can find that out. Make sure you don't nag him about his weight. His complaining about it could be a cry for reassurance.

Maybe he just needs encouragement—why don't you both work out together; even if you don't need to lose weight it will make you healthier and him happier. You could suggest he join Weight Watchers of NutraSystem or another diet center. But ultimately it's his decision and his will power that must get him through this. If he really doesn't want to lose weight, nothing you do will get him to.

Suggesting Alternatives to Intercourse

Q. I've been going out with my boyfriend for almost a year now. I used to touch him all the time, including grabbing him where it counts. But one day he told me I shouldn't touch him there unless I meant it. Now I don't touch him at all. How can I make it so I can touch him, but not have to have sex every time?

A. You need to open up your sexual relationship to include goals other than intercourse and climax. When the goal is always the same, then you always know where you're going—and that gets boring after a while.

So how do you let your boyfriend know this without offending him? Don't tell him what's wrong—tell him what you'd like to do with him. Next time he starts making sexual signals, suggest that there be a certain rule—like you can touch him, but he can't touch you. Or you have to do whatever you do standing up. Or that there will be no intercourse—just manual stimulation or rubbing against each other (use lotion, it's great). Stick to the rule for that encounter, and you'll find you have a completely unique sexual experience. By deliberately directing your encounter down a certain path, that shows both of you there are other ways of sexual interaction than intercourse. You have two complete bodies to work with—why stick to one or two variations of intercourse or oral sex when you can have something different every time?

If you can show your boyfriend that there are rewards other than intercourse, then it will be an easy jump to convince him that orgasm doesn't have to be the end result of every touch. This will bring your sexuality into the rest of your life. A kiss on the neck as you pass in the kitchen can be a complete sexual encounter. A naked hug after a shower is a wonderful sexual encounter. Show him how much richer his life is when you both have the excitement of not knowing exactly what will happen next.

Playing Second Fiddle

Q. I have a friend I like very much. He was in a long relationship that broke up six months ago, and he's been going out with another girl besides me for a few months. We've been going out about a month but we haven't had sex.

I'm not sure if he's having sex with the other girl or not. He carries a snapshot of both of them together in his wallet, and when I asked about her, he said she really helped him get over his depression when his last girlfriend left. What I want to know is should I have sex with him? Will that make him like me more than her?

A. If you have sex with him right now, it will just make *you* like him more and want more from him. Keep going out with him and let him know you're interested in developing your relationship, but in this case don't push him along. Let him turn to you. Be a good friend and get to know everything about him. Does he want the same sort of relationship you do? If he is interested in deepening your relationship, make sure he's giving you what you feel you need in both time and attention before you do. Otherwise, you'll feel used, and when he keeps spending time with the other girl you'll probably be jealous.

Orgasms

Q. It may sound weird, but sometimes when my boyfriend and I are making love, I don't think he's really into it. Sometimes he comes great, and other times it doesn't seem very intense for him. When I ask he says he liked it, but he doesn't want to talk about it and changes the subject. What do I do?

A. Don't your orgasms vary in intensity? If they don't, you're really missing out on something. Actually, it doesn't sound like you have a physical problem here, but an emotional one on your part. If he's not complaining, then no one's keeping score. Why is it so important to you? Why won't he talk to you about it? Have you considered that it might be your own insecurities on the subject that are keeping him silent? Maybe he'd like to discuss his various kinds of orgams with you, but he doesn't want to let you know when it was simply a roll-over good feeling when you make it clear you want him to be in the throes of ecstasy every time. Ego gets in the way of a lot of good sex.

Initiating sex

Q. I've been married for three years, and my husband rarely makes the first move when it comes to sex. I used to when we first got together, but I guess I sort of slacked off. I wish he was more aggressive. But when I try to tell him that, he says that I'm always busy when he wants to. That can't be true always. How can I get him to be more aggressive?

A. Tell your husband that for the next coming week you aren't going to initiate sex at all—that it's up to him. If he doesn't want to, then you won't have sex. The week after that it's your turn to initiate. If you want to have sex, then you can suggest it. Do that for five or six weeks and you both should form the habit of switching back and forth when it comes to initiating sex.

Both a Liar and an Adulterer

Q. I've been going out with a guy for eight months and I just found out he's married. He never told me in eight months. A friend at work found out and told me. I met him at work and we were friends and then started dating. We had a good sexual relationship, I thought. He didn't see me very much, but he always called me. He says that his marriage is over and that he'll be leaving her and that he really loves me. I believe him about that, but this whole thing bothers me.

A. It should bother you. Do not, not ever, trust a man who would lie to you for eight months about something as serious as his marriage. If he had told you from the beginning that he was married and the relationship was disintegrating, I would have said—well, maybe. But to lie to you this whole time! Forget the guy. There are more problems there than you want to deal with.

Only Sex

Q. I've been dating a man for eight months now. We have sex a lot, every time we see each other. He says he loves me, but once we have sex he draws away and doesn't pay much attention to me anymore. He's got three room-mates and their friends are always over at the house. We usually hang out with them. They talk about girls in front of me sometimes, among themselves, and it's so sexual. How can I get my boyfriend to do other things with me alone?

A. By not having sex every time you see him. It sounds to me like you need to know if he wants to be with you for you or for the sex. If it's only for sex, then you need to ask yourself if that's enough for you.

Tell your boyfriend you want to go out together. Go to a restaurant or movie or just walk and talk. If he won't, then tell him *you* are going whether he comes or not. Then do it, even if he doesn't come with you. Don't see him for the rest of the night and definitely don't have sex with him. Do this a few times over a couple weeks. If he consistently refuses to do what you want, but continues the same pattern other nights, then you have to face facts. Do you want a man who doesn't care about your needs and desires? Do you want to give someone so selfish your precious time and love? If he can't give to your needs, then don't hesitate. Leave him so you can find someone who can.

Younger Man

Q. I'm forty-two and have two children in their late teens. I've been dating a man who is thirty-two for almost a year. Honestly, when the affair started I didn't expect much. He's very nice, and our sex life suits me just fine. He likes my kids, but he never seemed interested in becoming a father to them, and I didn't blame him. He's ten years younger than I am. I expected him to drift away after a while. But last week he proposed to me. I knew he seemed happy with our life together, but I couldn't believe it. In all consciousness, I'm not sure that I can accept his offer. I can't have kids anymore, and that would mean he wouldn't have kids. And what if he marries me and after a couple years starts seeing signs of age he didn't expect?

A. It sounds to me like has has freely made his own choice in the matter. You made no indications that you would leave if he didn't marry you. You expected nothing from him and didn't push him in any direction. You simply had a good time with him, and now he's telling you that he wants to continue having a good life with you.

As long as you've told him that you can't have children, then it is up to him to decide on that matter as well. You could still adopt or foster a child if you both want to. And as for your children, as long as his relationship is cordial at the very least, then it can grow naturally from there once he's a constant part of your family.

As for your age and signs of aging—you've already gotten the strongest assurance that he loves you for who you are.

Index